Waldo E. Rosebush in His Shop

AMERICAN FIREARMS
and the
CHANGING FRONTIER

Written by
WALDO E. ROSEBUSH
for the
Eastern Washington State Historical Society

Drawings by Ronald Kuhler

Eastern Washington State Historical Society
Spokane, Washington
1962

(Publication No. 1)

Printed in Spokane, Washington, by Litho-Art Printers

This publication is posthumously published and dedicated to the memory of its author WALDO E. ROSEBUSH by the Eastern Washington State Historical Society. In recent years this modest man provided valuable counsel and assistance in assembling, restoring, and preserving the Society's Gun Collection which is on display in the Cheney Cowles Memorial Museum, Spokane, Washington.

PREFATORY NOTE

In describing the historical and mechanical development of fire-arms, the main effort of this booklet will be to emphasize those made or used in North America. The conquest of the New World in North America, and the accompanying 250-year struggle by competing interests for the resources and opportunities there, had a world-wide influence on the development of new weapons, especially in later years. Today these veteran American weapons are the visual contacts we have of the inventive genius and decisive events of a bygone day.

This booklet was published principally for the thousands of visitors, especially students, who come monthly to the Society's Museum. Its content, scope, and arrangement were given much study by Florence D. Reed, Director Emeritus, and Betty W. Bender, Librarian of the Society. After the author's untimely death in November, 1961, these two ladies completed the work still unfinished. Without their valuable suggestions and hours of work, both with Mr. Rosebush and after his death, this booklet might never have been completed. The illustrations were drawn by Ronald Kuhler, Curator of History. They were prepared principally from specimens in the Society's collections.

Acknowledgements are due also to Somerset Maugham, for use of the quotation on page 87, to the Pennsylvania Historical and Museum Commission for use of the illustration on page 20, and to the Macmillan Company for permission to use the quotation on page 32.

Richard Conn, Director

TABLE OF CONTENTS

LIST OF ILLUSTRATIONS

BIOGRAPHICAL NOTE

Waldo E. Rosebush's interest in guns began when he was a young boy and continued throughout his entire life. The initial interest undoubtedly stemmed from hearing men relate their experiences of opening the West and participating in Civil War battles.

He was born in Alfred, New York, on March 2, 1889, and was graduated from Alfred University. Alfred was and still is a small university town ten miles from the nearest railroad. When he was a boy it was a Seventh Day Baptist Community. Life there was a close knit family and religious one. This background remained a part of him throughout his life, and it was evident in his strong love for family ties and the traditions of a puritan type upbringing and heritage. He had strong patriotic feelings and at heart was a soldier all his life. This no doubt was due to his service in the army during World War I. Whenever the flag marched by he would come to stiff attention with a look that reflected the memory of the war.

Prior to army service he was a high school teacher in Wisconsin and also coached football and baseball. He then went into the paper business in Appleton, Wisconsin, until he left for service in the army with the Wisconsin National Guard, having received his commission as Second Lieutenant in the Infantry. The Guard unit was sent to the Mexican border where he served under General Pershing (1916-1917) and then on to France (1917-1920). He received the Pershing Merit Citation with the Purple Heart. At the close of World War I he held the rank of Major in the United States Infantry.

After the war he returned to Wisconsin and then on to Millwood, Washington, where he became, in time, mill manager and treasurer of Inland Empire Paper Co., during the period of 1922-1938.

In 1938 he retired from this work and spent the next five years working on private matters which included guns and inventions some of which he patented. Early in World War II he attempted to get back into army service but his age made this impossible. He finally contributed his part to the war effort by taking a position in charge of base construction in the Aleutian Islands where he remained until 1951, serving under three branches of the armed services — Army, Navy, and Air Corps.

When he returned to the states he went back to his hobby of collecting and making guns, searching for a design which could be produced inexpensively and which would handle a variety of ammunition. He was a genius with guns and his many creations show a skill in design and craftmanship that could certainly classify him as a gunmaker and an artisan of the old school. A group of weapons which he invented and built are on display in the Museum of the State Historical Society of Wisconsin in Madison. In this Museum, there is also a gun collection assembled over a period of 50 years by Waldo E. Rosebush and his brother Franz.

In his personal life he was frugal and his personal wants were few. He maintained an active interest in political, economic, and historical matters up to the time of his death in 1961. He appreciated fine arts and music, and he was especially interested in American history. The pioneer spirit that built America was ever near the surface in this man.

E.W.S.H.S.

CHAPTER I

FLASHES THAT CHANGED THE WORLD

THE FIRST FLASHES ON THE FIRST FRONTIER

The development of firearms from the mortar-and-pestle gunpowder of the alchemist started in Europe about the 13th century. It came just in time to reinforce the drastic breakup of the feudal system initiated by the English longbow.

How did man discover gunpowder and the means to apply it to projectiles? Naturally the projectile came first — almost with man's origin. In Biblical history, a stone was the lethal weapon used by Cain to kill his brother Abel. Later came knives, spears, the javelin, and the bow and arrow. The latter definitely created studies of ballistics or the nature and characteristics of missiles in flight as affected by the initial force of propulsion, opposed by the pull of gravity. Finally, certain savage tribes devised the blowgun which embodies the principle of the firearm: air suddenly expelled from the lungs, applied to a pellet or dart in the tube; and the tube accurately controlling the line of flight to the target.

But to make an effective firearm, man required several primary things. The most important was fire. Lightning from the heavens brought him the miracle of fire. He needed the wheel which was suggested by rolling rocks and fallen tree trunks. He needed the lever indicated in various ways: by eating, or by the use of arms and legs; by uprooted trees; by poles lodged across fallen tree trunks; or by spars of driftwood wedged in rocks and broken off short by streams in flood. The retractive spring was suggested by the tree branches on which he swung or the brush he pushed through, eventually resulting in the bow and arrow. And he was to find even greater benefit from all of these devices in other ways, of which transportation and construction are good examples.

Fire permitted man to concentrate and purify the minerals found in rocks. Thus he was able to produce lead, copper, tin, other soft metals, and finally iron. Fire enabled man to do many things with iron, one of the most important being that he could harden it into steel. And with rocks of pyrites or flint striking the steel, he found that he could make the same fire first brought to him from the clouds and do it easier than he could by the frictional means of rubbing wood on wood.

Also, he discovered that fire was intense oxidation. Therefore by using hides as an airchamber — a bellows — he was able to intensify the fire which made possible the easy shaping and welding of iron and the making of better steel — not to mention other important new processes and discoveries.

In his further quest for minerals on the land, man discovered sulphur and, much later, saltpeter. As early as the 3rd century B.C., he was delving into chemical combinations with sulphur and other elements which caused combustion liberating large quantities of burning gas. One very early combination of the 5th century B.C. was Greek fire, a relatively slow burning combustible used in naval combat and in battles for walled cities.

Then one day in the 13th century A.D., there was an explosion and gunpowder was born. Where this first occurred is unknown.[1] It may have been in Spain or Germany, or it may have been in England where Roger Bacon cryptically recorded certain discoveries characteristic of gunpowder. One legend indicates that the explosion took place in the grinding of mortar and pestle when a spark set off the mixture of sulphur, saltpeter, and charcoal; and it blew the pestle violently out of the hand. Quite as likely is the possibility that a mixture of sulphur and saltpeter was dropped or thrown on hot embers, a combination which, even with varying proportions, would burn violently. But as the mixture was studied and improved and a cannon built to use it, the name mortar for a very short-barreled cannon continued to carry the implication of the origin of gunpowder as in the first theory above. With the shallow cannon or mortar and the blowgun in mind, there was required only a means for making metal tubes strong enough to contain a powder charge and projectiles for manual use.

The cannon was first fired with a slow match or wick inserted from the muzzle. Soon after, a better method was employed by use of a small hole from the outside of the piece leading directly to the base of the powder charge in the bore. So from the beginning, this was the method of firing used in all hand or shoulder firearms, except for changes in systems of ignition to be explained next.

[1]Of reputed similar discoveries in China about the same time, there does not appear to be any definite authentic record. Actually, gunpowder, as we know it, was a very slow development rather than a sudden discovery. And it did not become effective until man found out how to make pure saltpeter — potassium nitrate.

THE DEVELOPMENT OF IGNITION SYSTEMS

If one considers all the variations in the methods or mechanics of ignition, including the modern metallic cartridge first employed martially in America during the Civil War, there are perhaps thirteen such systems. But the essential changes in the progression number eight,[2] with the approximate periods during which they operated or overlapped, being as follows:

1. Hand cannon — 1350 to 1800. (Its late use was in China and Japan)
2. Matchlock or firelock — 1450 to 1850. (Its late use was in the Orient)
3. Wheellock — 1500 to 1700.
4. Snaphance or snaphaunce — 1550-70 to 1700.
5. Miquelet — 1575 to 1750.
6. Flintlock — 1615 to 1850.
7. Percussion lock — 1817 onward.
8. Metallic cartridge — 1836 onward.

The earlier dates given above are approximations which are based on various old writings.

Let us examine first the hand cannon and the four early systems of ignition because these developments were used more in Europe than in America. Then, in succeeding chapters, the flintlock, percussion lock, and metallic cartridge will be illustrated and explained with the discussion of the American developments.

HAND CANNON, 1350. — The hand cannon was made in two forms both having the fire vent or touchhole at the rear of the tube or barrel. To enable the charge to be fired readily, a cup-shaped cavity was formed around the vent into the barrel so that a small pinch of powder placed therein would be readily accessible to a glowing match

---

[2]The other five ignition systems are variations. The matchlock is sometimes classified in three stages, i.e. the lever or serpentine operated by pressing it with a finger and manually retracted; the spring retracted serpentine; and the first actual gunlock whereby the serpentine is triggered by a spring-controlled lever.

The remaining three systems are of the flint type: the Scandinavian in which the battery or frizzen may be turned to one side as a safety; the English dog-lock which provides another type of safety; and the Mediterranean lock (similar to the Miquelet) of Spanish or Italian workmanship. The Miquelet has a replaceable face for the battery to compensate for wear by the striking flint which, with each stroke, scrapes off incandescent bits of steel to fire the priming powder.

or hot wire. The first form, illustrated below, was affixed to a long handle which could be supported underneath the holding arm, while the other arm and hand touched off the powder charge with a red-hot wire, burning piece of punk, tinder or "slow match."

Hand Cannon

The second form seems to have been almost exclusively Oriental, consisting of the metal barrel held in one hand while being fired by slow match with the other. This piece was usually small, quite short, but having a fairly large bore. It appears more suited to celebrations than for any lethal purpose.

MATCHLOCK OR FIRELOCK, 1450. — Because of its simplicity, the matchlock or as often called in American military terminology, the firelock, lasted in the Orient for several hundred years.

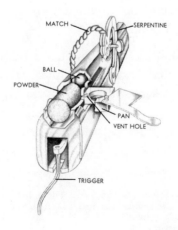

Matchlock

The long goose-necked or serpentine bar carried at its upper end the lighted match which could be brought surely in contact with the powder at the priming vent with one swift stroke. At first, the lower end of this bar was pressed by a finger to bring the match down in contact with the powdered vent. Following this, a spring was added so that, when finger pressure was released, the bar resumed its upright position. In its final form about 100 years later, there was a lock including a trigger which, operating separately, released the serpentine bar. This bar, actuated by its spring, snapped down to contact the match with the priming powder. A principal handicap was the lighted match which especially at night gave warning.

WHEELLOCK, 1500. — While the wheellock provided a much more certain and effective means of ignition than its predecessors, it was so complicated and expensive that only people of some means or wealth could afford one. Therefore the wheellocks preserved today show more inlay work, engraving, and other artistic embellishment than later firearms. Also, because of their cost and artistic value, they did not overlap in point of time or period of use to the extent shown by either their predecessors or the less complicated and cheaper systems which followed them. Their high cost becomes understandable when the mechanical operation, as explained below, is considered.

In or on the lockplate was a wheel with a roughened rim. This wheel was connected with a very strong spring wound up crank fashion until caught and held by bars connected with a trigger beneath the grip of the stock. Above the wheel on the lockplate was a pan through the bottom of which the wheel rotated when released. This pan had a slidable cover so that priming powder placed in the pan would be retained in movement and thus covered kept fairly dry from light rain. The pan rested also against the side of the barrel and connected directly with the vent leading to the powder charge in the "bore" which is the term applied to the inside of the barrel. Forward of the pan was an angular bar with its upper end suggestive of the jaws of a dog. And in the dog's mouth was a piece of iron pyrites or flint. The angular bar, with this piece of pyrites or flint, rocked on an axis above a strong spring which exerted its greatest pressure when the bar was in either forward position or backward with the pyrites or flint resting on the priming pan cover. While in this position, if the trigger was pulled or released, it freed the wheel which then revolved at a rapid rate, at the same time drawing back the pan cover which then allowed the pyrites or flint under the strong pressure of its spring to drop on the wheel. This caused sparks to fly like a grinding wheel thereby igniting the priming powder which flamed through the vent to explode the charge in the barrel. The main defect in this operation was the need for a key or spanner crank to wind the wheel spring. If the key or spanner was lost, the gun was useless.

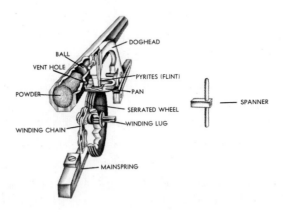

Wheellock

SNAPHANCE, 1550. — The shaphance (also snaphaunce) is said to have been originated by the Dutch who called it *snaphaans* meaning chicken thieves; or by the Germans who called it *schnapp hahn* meaning a pecking hen. The chicken thieves were supposed to have devised this means of ignition to avoid carrying (and thus revealing themselves) the lighted match of the matchlock. The pecking hen idea seems to have come from the appearance of the bar carrying the flint, so suggestive of a fighting rooster — hence the name "cock." In any event it was a far simpler and cheaper means of ignition than the wheellock.

The bar which held the flint, the so-called cock, was now at the rear of the pan on the outside of the lockplate. A rocking piece inside had an integral shaft which rotated in a round hole in the lockplate; and its square outer end fitted a corresponding hole in the axial end of the cock which was held rigidly to the shaft by a screw. The rocking piece, termed the tumbler, engaged by a strong spring, was held in striking or cocked position by a bar called a sear. This sear could be released at will by a trigger on the underside of the gunstock. In the same relative way as the wheellock, the lockplate held a pan for the priming powder and also had a similar cover. As first conceived, when ready to fire, the pan was manually moved forward out of the way of the cock thus exposing the priming powder. Later, the movement of the pan was automatically done by a bar connected with the tumbler which shot it forward when the trigger was pulled and the cock fell. Above the pan was an angular piece called the battery or frizzen against which the cock-held flint struck a glancing blow as it fell, causing sparks to ignite priming powder and fire the gun.

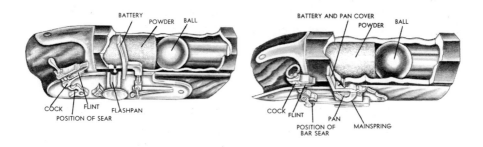

Snaphance   Miquelet

MIQUELET, 1575. — The miquelet was very similar to the snaphance, the most striking difference being that the mainspring was placed on the outside of the lockplate, thus acting directly on the cock which, by a bar-sear through a hole in the lockplate, was held in striking position until released by the trigger below. Perhaps also it was the first of the flint family to combine the pan cover and the battery or frizzen into one angular piece as will be explained more specifically when we discuss the next step — the regulation flintlock. It should be said now, however, that the miquelet battery was L-shaped while the flintlock battery was curved in order to receive a more oblique or scraping blow from the flint. The scraping action removed tiny particles of steel and like a circular grindstone made them incandescent.

CHAPTER II

COLONIAL AMERICA

Early American colonists from England, France, Switzerland, Germany (the Palatinate), Austria, Belgium, Holland, Spain, usually brought with them the firearm common to their own country. Some of the colonists, lacking firearms or ammunition, also used the Indian bow and arrow as the English had done so effectively at Crecy, Poitiers, and Agincourt 300 to 350 years before. Sometimes, too, in getting game, the arrow was more advantageous because it made no noise and it carried no lighted match, as required by the matchlock gun, to scare the game or advise Indian enemies of the location of white hunters.

THE PENNSYLVANIA RIFLE, ca. 1730

The German and Swiss immigrants, who settled in eastern Pennsylvania during the forepart of the 18th century, brought with them their large-calibered, *rifled* hunting guns which, from this use, they called "Jaegers." Rifling is the grooving, usually spiral, in the bore of the gun to spin the ball so that it will fly straight and true to the line of sighting. Due to the demands of the backwoods hunter, these Jaegers were rapidly improved into the small-calibered, comparatively light Pennsylvania rifle with a long barrel. The best of these rifles were deadly accurate at 300 paces. In this way originated the famous "American Rifle" as fifty years later it came to be called in Europe. By the next century in America, it was commonly called the "Kentucky" rifle because of its use by noted explorers across that "dark and bloody ground" — by many considered not so much a state as a vast wild Indian region.

The muskets, used in all wars of the world up to and including our Civil War, were of large caliber — that is to say, the bore or hole in the barrel was large, sometimes (as in the American Revolution) more than three-quarters of an inch in diameter. Therefore they could be used as shotguns for rabbits, birds, or other small game, as readily as they were used with the heavy single balls for bear, deer, or other large animals. But even with the single ball, the accurate range of these smoothbores was short — usually no farther than a baseball player can throw a ball.

CARTRIDGES

Since the latter part of the 16th century, cartridges for all military muskets had been made by placing the powder and lead ball within a capsule of paper. This facilitated the rapid loading of guns in battle. Thus the idea was primarily military though the practice was not limited to soldiers except for the means and inclination or need for making cartridges.

Generally, the loading of firearms was directly from powder horn and bullet pouch suspended on the right hip by thongs carried over the left shoulder. The powder horns were made from the horns of home-butchered cattle and the bullet pouches from deerskin. Their use still continues in many places in the world today with muzzle-loading weapons for economy, for hunting, or for a hobby. If using a single ball for game, the old method for determining the proper charge was to place the ball on the upturned palm of the hand and pour powder from the horn upon it until the ball was covered. A short tip of another cow horn was then prepared to take, at full level, this identical amount of powder. Then the small measuring horn was attached by a thong to the powder horn for permanent use with the gun.

If cartridges were used, the soldier bit off the folded end, poured some powder into the pan, dumped the remainder down the barrel, and rammed down the ball; sometimes, if shooting downward, adding the wadded paper on top of the ball to keep it from rolling out.

THE FLINTLOCK, 1615-1850, SUPERSEDES
ALL EARLIER TYPES

The Pilgrim Fathers and other early Colonials used many match-locks, wheellocks, and snaphances. During King William's War, 1689-1697, and Queen Anne's War, 1713, except for the snaphances, relatively few appear to have remained in active use. The continued contest between the English and the French — King George's War, 1744-1748, and the French and Indian War, 1754-1763 (the American part ending in 1760) — provided even less evidence of the matchlock and wheellock in active use. By that time, the simpler and cheaper flintlock was in use everywhere. Many British muskets had been brought to America to arm the Colonial militia for its support and help in these wars. Also during this period, the Pennsylvania Germans and Swiss were commencing to gain a reputation for their remarkable rifle which was to have such an effect on the future of America. This was a flintlock as illustrated below.

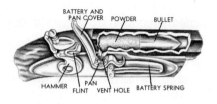

Flintlock

As may be readily noted, the flintlock is an improved snaphance. For more than 200 years it performed a vast and fairly reliable service. Even today it still finds sporadic use. Flintlocks for the African trade were made even later than the year 1900 because, in the African bush country, flints were easier and cheaper to obtain than copper percussion caps. The flintlock, by combining the battery or frizzen and pan cover into one angular piece, provided a simpler, more rugged lock than the snaphance and at less cost. The flintlock sear engaged directly the tumbler safety and firing notches. The longer backward curve of the battery was easier on the flint and seemed to give a better spray of sparks. And the free blow of the cock seemed to open the pan quicker and throw back the battery faster than did the snaphance. This lock played a most important part in the world's history.

FUR TRADE AND THE TRADE GUN, 1650-1875

The American Indians obtained their first firearms from the 17th century fur traders in New England and New York. These traders sometimes made 1000 per cent in exchanging guns, powder, and shot or bullets for pelts brought in by the Indians. Because the profits were so high, it was extremely difficult to keep firearms from reaching the hands of even the recognized hostile Indians. In 1641, the British Crown issued an order prohibiting this trade in guns. Nevertheless, because of competition between the Dutch, the English, and the French, some of the fur traders continued the barter, knowing full well that these same guns might be used against women and children along the frontier even to the smaller settlements.[1]

By the middle of the 17th century, the Dutch along the Hudson River had an established gun trade with the Indians. The English, moving westward from the colonies on the eastern seaboard and seeking to extend their trade with the Indians, soon became strong rivals both to the Dutch and to the French on the St. Lawrence. As one result, this meant that the Indian's preference of the type of gun to be had became a factor in the fur trade. Thus, by the end of the 17th century, the short musket (*mousquet*) of the French, called a *fusil,* or, as pronounced generally by all three competitors, the "fusee", already was favored by the Indians. In addition, the French were giving the Indians better bargains in trade, i.e. asking fewer beaver skins for the guns and ammunition. So the Dutch and the English also had to supply a short, light musket in order to maintain their trade.

As pointed out earlier, by this time the flintlock was common everywhere because the armies of Europe as early as 1650 had adopted it generally, and all the colonists in America (English, French, and Dutch in the north; and the Spanish in Florida and on the lower Mississippi) were receiving them. But, regardless of the quantities of trade guns supplied to the Indians from all these sources, the colonial wars, soon to develop on a large scale, would far overshadow the fur trade means of arming the Indians. By making allies of these Indians in the wars, they had to be given firearms outright by the English and the French; and through the agency of the latter, particularly along the western waterways, by 1750 the use of the flintlock had reached almost to the western plains.

THE HUDSON'S BAY COMPANY. — In 1670, Charles II, King of England, granted to Prince Rupert and seventeen other gentlemen a charter to enjoy the sole trade and commerce into Hudson's Bay and contiguous waters.[2] Due to the French occupation of the St. Lawrence and Great Lakes waterways, the operation of this English chartered

---

[1]This is an example of the unconscionable avarice afflicting mankind throughout all ages up to this day. One would sell his soul for a dollar, recently known as a "fast buck", tainted with unfairness if not the blood of other people. Another would accept without protest the profit of a shady deal if he himself was not involved personally.

[2]This charter was finally relinquished to the Crown in 1869. In return, the Hudson's Bay Company received as compensation from the Dominion of Canada, 300,000 pounds sterling for Rupert's Land, but retained with rights of trade all its posts and stations, plus a considerable "fertile land" tenure.

Hudson's Bay Company was quite limited until after the formal end of the war between France and England by the Treaty of Paris in 1763. Thereafter, the Company's fur trading operations with the Indians expanded tremendously. For this business, shortly before the American Revolution, the Company commenced to supply a short, smoothbore trade gun made for the trade. This gun was a close-range piece but very suitable for hunting due to the Indian's method of quiet stalking. But there is no evidence that the so-called "Hudson's Bay Gun", with the dragon or serpentine side-plate, large trigger guard, and fox symbols stamped on the lockplate or barrel, became standard until about 1800.

CONQUEST OF THE NEW WORLD

During the last half of the 17th century, the struggle for North America entered a decisive phase. The Swedes in New Jersey were absorbed by the Dutch of New York in 1655; and the Dutch surrendered to the English in 1665. In the last quarter of the century began the 100-year, intensive struggle between the English and the French all over the world. Finally Montreal and all of Canada were surrendered to the English General Amherst in September, 1760, largely due to Wolfe's great victory one year earlier at Quebec. In 1763 Spain ceded Florida to the English. But Spain, drifting under various shifts of fortune, would not be eliminated in the south for another sixty years.

As a general grouping of these vastly important trends and relationships between the leading nations of those times, a brief approximation might focus events in this way: the 16th century marked Spain's conquest of South America and the lands bordering the Gulf of Mexico; the 17th century saw the colonization of North America by the English, the French, the Dutch, and the Swedes, with the last two absorbed by the English; the 18th century ended with the English triumphant over France and Spain, but having lost, to become an independent nation, her thirteen colonies south of the St. Lawrence River.

FIREARMS DURING THE LATE COLONIAL PERIOD

From her colonies England wanted only raw materials for which she would send in exchange the manufactured products. The Pennsylvania rifle was not a suitable gun for England but, generally speaking, the growth of home industry in America was slower than normal for quality products; and British muskets arrived in volume when wars with the French threatened. The effect of this was not so much to prevent the Pennsylvania rifle from becoming a military weapon as it was to discourage gunsmiths in general from trying to make and sell military muskets in competition with the British weapons. As a result, when the American Revolution came, there were no American-made muskets to be had. Although there were several hundred gunsmiths in the country, they were makers of pieces for individuals who wanted light guns of a particular type for hunting and general use and naturally without the bayonet which then was a prime military necessity.

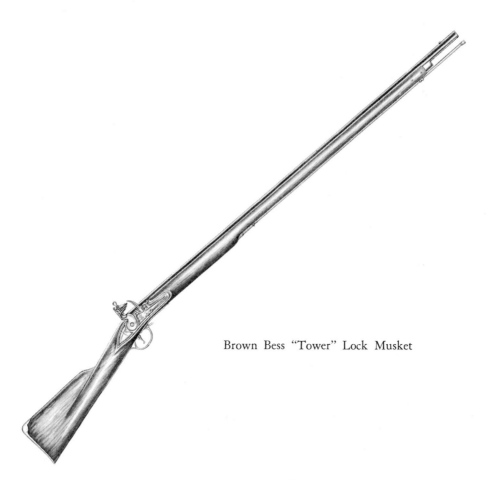

Brown Bess "Tower" Lock Musket

BROWN BESS, 1718-1794.[3] — The "Brown Bess" was the regulation musket of the British Empire from the later Colonial wars
until about 1794. It was a smoothbore of roughly .75 caliber, a sturdy
piece orginally weighing 14 pounds, with a barrel from 42 to 46 inches
long. In participating in the English-French wars in America, the Colonial militia received many of these muskets and thus they formed a
nucleus of the various kinds of weapons used in the American Revolution. They were copied by American gunsmiths so far as they could
in producing muskets for that war.

However, because of its comparatively short range and inaccuracy,
this weapon was not very effective in Indian fighting. For that sort of
work the Pennsylvania rifle was supreme. George Washington's backwoodsmen used the latter to save the 400 men of Braddock's command
near Fort Duquesne in 1755. Firing from behind trees, Washington's
men made their carefully aimed shots count dead Indians while the
English in close order, volley firing with European regularity in the
open, with the big-mouthed Brown Bess smoothbores aimed blindly
at the forest, were cut down like cattle in a slaughter pen by the forest-
hidden Indians and French.[4]

Again, five years later in the advance to the "Plains of Abraham"
at Quebec, the English, wiser this time, placed companies of Pennsylvania provincials armed with their own rifles at the very front of the
advance to cut down the French skirmishers. This cleared the way for
the British regulars who drove home the attack and won from the
French all of Canada for the British Empire. General Wolfe of the
British, three times struck and mortally wounded in the fight, when
told of his victory, murmured, "Now God be praised, I die content".

---

[3]American firearms collectors have in the past sometimes assumed that the Brown Bess
was the regulation British musket from 1710-15 to the adoption of the Enfield rifle midway
of the 19th century, after limited use of the Baker, Brunswick and Lovell rifles. But those
who specialize in early British weapons, consider the Brown Bess as the regulation musket
only until 1794. During this period it underwent minor changes including a reduction in
barrel length to 42 inches. Also the stock and mountings were lightened which with the
shortened barrel combined to reduce the weight of the musket two pounds in spite of the
replacement of the wood ramrod with one of steel. The powder pan was provided with a bridle
which strengthened the operation of the battery or frizzen. After 1794 the India pattern
musket was adopted. This was a still lighter and cheaper version of the Brown Bess. It had
a 39-inch barrel and thus the ram pipes could be reduced from four to three. This musket
was about the same weapon formerly used by the East India Company. It was used in the
War of 1812 and for several decades thereafter.

[4]The Iroquois are said to have used the flintlock rifle about the same time; and Dillin
quotes Auguste Chouteau as stating that the Chickasaw Indians were armed with the rifle and
generally were good shots with it as early as 1736.

BACKWOODS RIFLE. — While the Pennsylvania (Kentucky) rifle, with few exceptions,[5] was not made primarily for military use — because the rifled barrel was more expensive and slower to load than the smoothbore musket in which the ball fitted loosely and because it was not designed for the bayonet — nevertheless it was the principal occupational firearm of the flintlock era in the English colonies of North America. By 1750, its fame and worth had been well demonstrated from Savannah to the St. Lawrence, and already it was winning a name in the wilderness west of the Shenandoah. Also before the Revolution, it would be on the march with Daniel Boone into Kentucky. Other events connected with it are yet to be mentioned.[6]

FRENCH CHARLEVILLE MUSKET. — In the wars with the French along the northern and western borders, some of the weapons they used had been captured and examined. It was observed that these firearms had some elements of superiority for military use, particularly their late model musket of 1763. Therefore when the American Revolution gradually cast its shadow, this French musket was remembered because France, having been long at odds with England, very likely would not only be willing but anxious to help the American colonies by supplying weapons in case of war.

[5] See footnote and related text on page 25.

[6] As a comparison, during the 100 years preceding 1763, the French trade with the Indians along the St. Lawrence and western waterways has been estimated to amount to a total of 200,000 guns from France. More than 100,000 muskets were absorbed by English regulars, militiamen, and Indian allies during the French and Indian War. These ranged from antiquated matchlocks to the Brown Bess musket and the shorter fusee preferred by the Indians. Many matchlock guns were refitted with flint locks.

CHAPTER III

THE AMERICAN REVOLUTION

When in 1775 the Revolution came and Americans were scurrying for firearms of every kind, France did indeed come to the aid of the Colonists and so did helpful Frenchmen like Lafayette.[1] In this way the French Charleville musket, illustrated below, became one of our most reliable infantry muskets along with the confiscated stocks of the British Brown Bess and, in the hands of hunters and backwoodsmen,

French Charleville Musket

[1]France supplied on one agreement 24,000 muskets with bayonets and other accoutrements.

the ubiquitous Pennsylvania rifle. Many muskets or guns of a military type for bayonets were supplied by private gunmakers in the colonies though some were of doubtful quality. But it was hard to make and maintain standards in a hurry, so the private output varied in many ways in spite of all that Committees of Safety could do. These committees were formed in each colonial division and charged with arming and equipping the soldiers they supplied.

In April, 1775, there was a quarrel with Lord Dunmore, the detested Governor of Virginia ("Dunmore's War" of the preceding year), about his seizure of the powder in the magazine at Williamsburg. Patrick Henry headed a delegation which called on the Governor and got $1500 in payment. Some of Dunmore's letters misrepresenting the Colonists were intercepted, and this aggravated the situation so much that he took refuge on a British vessel, declared martial law, and asked slaves to leave their masters and support him. In November, the Virginia militia came to defend the approach to Norfolk. Then Dunmore, with his seamen and sundry cohorts, arrived to drive them out. The seamen bravely charged down a narrow causeway 160 yards long at the end of which were the entrenched Virginians. The fire of these sharpshooters was terrific. The British leader Fordyce fell, struck by fourteen balls. The rest fled leaving half their number behind. The Virginians lost none, only one being slightly wounded.

1775: VALOR MEETS VALOR AT BOSTON
HUNTING GUN vs. MUSKET

The first real test of the American patriots came at Breed's Hill near Boston, June 17, 1775, popularly called the Battle of Bunker Hill. On the hillside were 1500 undisciplined countrymen, weary from throwing up breastworks during the night, hungry, thirsty, and under an untested leader. At the waterside were 3000 picked troops richly uniformed and equipped — officers and men who had been victorious on many famous European battlefields. The neighboring hills, and the streets and roofs of Boston, were crowded with anxious spectators. The British, in solid, red-coated ranks, slowly marched up the hill to the measured tap of the drums, breaking ranks only to throw down fences and pass other obstructions. As they drew near they fired massed volleys, rank by rank, while all the British ships and floating batteries in the nearby harbor rained shot and shell upon the patriot breastworks.

Prescott, commanding the Americans, ordered his men to hold fire until they could "see the whites of their eyes" and then to "aim at their waistbands." When the British closed to about fifty yards, Prescott gave the word "FIRE!"

There was a blazing crash and a lingering cloud of sulphurous, gray smoke from end to end of the patriot line. Whole platoons of red-coats went down before that terribly accurate blast from the countryside's antique gun collection of muskets, hunting guns, and fowling pieces. Another volley soon followed. Then still another. The survivors, unwilling to run, stood among the dead and wounded, paralyzed and bewildered by the shock. Then the bugle sounded recall and they fell back to the shore.

After a brief delay, the British commander Howe rallied his men and again they advanced, covered partly by the smoke of burning Charlestown which had been fired by his orders. Again the red line met the same deadly blast and again it recoiled.

Clinton now came with reinforcements from Boston and a third effort was made. The British soldiers, by order, threw off their knapsacks and moved at the quickstep with the word to depend only upon the bayonet. British artillery fire was concentrated on one spot, and the defenders were driven into a redoubt which the British at once attacked on three sides. Since the Americans had little ammunition, only one heavy volley now met the head of the British advance which it tore to pieces; but the British ranks behind swarmed over the ramparts, their bayonets driving all before them. Even so, the patriots sturdily resisted. Few had bayonets so the others clubbed their guns and disputed every foot of ground. The redoubt was soon lost but the British, wounded and exhausted, were unable to continue the pursuit. They had lost 1000 men, the Americans 450. The dead lay "thick as sheep in the field".

On June 23, 1775, Washington set out for Cambridge to take command of his army.[2] He found it to number about 14,000, but it was an army only in name. In fact, it was a "gathering of neighbors, schoolmates and friends", each with his own gun, powder horn and bag of bullets, and only such provisions as he had brought with him. Powder

---

[2]In *Diary of the American Revolution* by Frank Moore (New York, 1860) is an extract taken from *Rivington's Gazette*, June 29, 1775, reading: "June 24. Yesterday morning General Washington and General Lee set off from Philadelphia to take command of the American Army at Massachusetts Bay . . . ."

was so scarce that there was only enough to average nine loads per man. "Almost the whole powder of the army was in the cartridge boxes."[3]

BACKWOODSMEN AND THE PENNSYLVANIA RIFLE IN THE REVOLUTION

The first troops raised under the order of Congress were the Virginia riflemen, twelve companies having come on foot from 400 to 800 miles. Says Bancroft, "The men painted in the guise of savages, were strong and of great endurance, many more than six feet tall; they wore leggins and mocassins, an ash-colored hunting shirt with a double cape." Each one carried a rifle, a hatchet, a small axe, and a hunters knife. They could subsist on a little parched corn and game killed as they went along. At night, wrapped in their blankets, they willingly made a tree their canopy, the earth their bed. The rifle in their hands sent its ball with unerring precision a distance of two to three hundred yards. Their motto was "Liberty or Death." Newspapers of the day relate how they offered to shoot apples off one another's heads; how one man at sixty paces put eight balls through a paper the size of a dollar. Another stuck his knife into a tree and, firing, halved his bullet upon the edge.[4]

During the war the Pennsylvania rifle continued to make its mark, at least to the extent that the British War Office stated: "The settlers from the backwoods of America used their hunting rifles with so much effect that the only effective rejoinder was to pit rifle against rifle; for this purpose Jägers were recuited from the Continent." The Jägers (meaning hunters and foresters versed in the use of the German rifle) were the Hessians of the old-time schoolbooks or Duffy's Reader. Though they may have been recruited to "pit rifle against rifle" and not merely as mercenaries to replace British soldiers, among the thousands sent were many grenadiers and certain riff-raff that the German Province of Hesse could well spare. The cupidity and brutality of some of these men excited general detestation.

---

[3]Joel Dorman Steele and Esther Baker Steele, *Barnes' Popular History of the United States of America* (New York, 1914), p. 156. These quotations, (reported by Reed, Washington's Secretary) probably originated with Bancroft. The one on cartridge boxes is made in a figurative sense since the gathering is military. Former militiamen probably had cartridge boxes; the others, powder horn and bullet pouch.

[4]*Ibid.*, p. 157. See also James Thatcher, M.D., *Military Journal during the Revolutionary War,* 1775-1783 (diary) (Hartford, Conn., 1854).

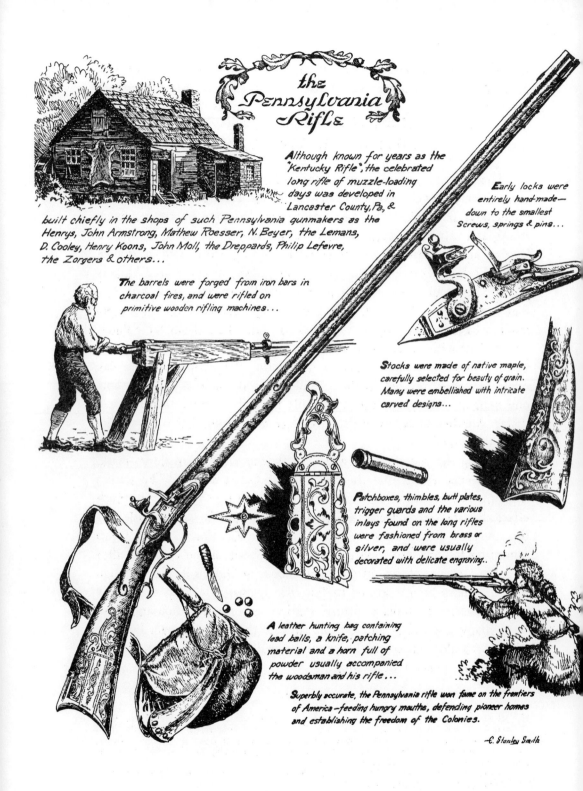

the Pennsylvania Rifle

Although known for years as the "Kentucky Rifle", the celebrated long rifle of muzzle-loading days was developed in Lancaster County, Pa, & built chiefly in the shops of such Pennsylvania gunmakers as the Henrys, John Armstrong, Mathew Roesser, N. Beyer, the Lemans, D. Cooley, Henry Koons, John Moll, the Dreppards, Philip Lefevre, the Zorgers & others...

Early locks were entirely hand-made — down to the smallest screws, springs & pins...

The barrels were forged from iron bars in charcoal fires, and were rifled on primitive wooden rifling machines...

Stocks were made of native maple, carefully selected for beauty of grain. Many were embellished with intricate carved designs...

Patchboxes, thimbles, butt plates, trigger guards and the various inlays found on the long rifles were fashioned from brass or silver, and were usually decorated with delicate engraving..

A leather hunting bag containing lead balls, a knife, patching material and a horn full of powder usually accompanied the woodsman and his rifle...

Superbly accurate, the Pennsylvania rifle won fame on the frontiers of America — feeding hungry mouths, defending pioneer homes and establishing the freedom of the Colonies.

—C. Stanley Smith

The Jäger or Hessian record in the war was not one in any way affecting the American backwoodsman and his rifle. In the strangeness of this country, the Hessians plundered some Royalist homes to the embarrassment of the British. And some deserted or otherwise ended British service to settle in Pennsylvania where they became good citizens.

As the year 1776 drew to a close, at the battle of Trenton, Hand's regiment of riflemen got in the rear of the Hessians and cut them off. Rall, the Hessian commander, was mortally wounded; and altogether Washington gathered in nearly 1000 prisoners, 1200 small arms, six guns, and all their standards.

The record of the rifle in the Revolution cannot be passed without mention of Daniel Morgan and his command. They took part in the abortive attack on Quebec in December, 1775. They had an important part in the capture of Burgoyne's army at Saratoga in 1777.[5] And at the Cowpens in January, 1781, Morgan, at the head of 900 men and officers, fought one of the best executed battles of the war when he cut Tarleton's force to pieces, losing only 72 while, besides the material of war, the British lost over 800, about one-sixth of Cornwallis' entire field army.

Finally, there is one other engagement of considerable importance because therein rifle met rifle. This was a fight which took place in the autumn preceding Morgan's well-executed Cowpens battle. It occurred at Kings Mountain, South Carolina, between 1200 or more American mounted backwoodsmen under Colonels Shelby and Sevier and 1100 men under Major Patrick Ferguson commanding the Second Battalion, 71st Regiment, Highland Light Infantry. Ferguson was the inventor of the Ferguson breech-loading flintlock rifle. Under Cornwallis, Ferguson's command was a raiding party about the same as Tarleton's. These raiding parties and the treatment they gave civilians had stirred up a lot of resentment and hate which was the reason these mounted backwoodsmen appeared bearing their own arms with gunpowder they had made at home and bullets they had cast on their own hearths.

Learning that the men from the hills were after him, Ferguson turned east toward the main army under Cornwallis. Nevertheless by hard riding the Americans caught up with Ferguson on Kings Mountain; and, regardless of the odds of position favoring him, they got their rifles going at once and in four concerted columns climbed up

[5]See footnote page 38.

the steep rocks from four sides, undeterred by repeated bayonet charges. About 100 of Ferguson's men were armed with his breech-loading rifle but that advantage appeared to make no difference. The contest had lasted an hour when Ferguson fell and his men surrendered. Four hundred and fifty-six of the British were killed and wounded, and 648 were taken prisoners. The Americans lost 88.

Officer's Custom-made Ferguson Rifle

Except for breech fouling, the Ferguson .60 caliber rifle had good possibilities as a flintlock breechloader.[6] One complete turn of the trigger guard unscrewed and opened the breech. Then, with muzzle down, a ball was dropped in and powder added from the powder horn. With the fresh load in the chamber, one turn of the guard back again closed the breech, and primed, the gun was ready to fire. But though the lock and breech were of finer craftsmanship, the Furguson rifle carried a .60 caliber ball as against the .35 to .50 caliber balls of the Pennsylvania product. It did not seem to be as adaptable; also there were too few of them to answer when those Carolina squirrel rifles commenced to pop with every shot hitting a target.

[6]Breechloaders had been a matter of experiment for over 200 years, but this was the first breechloader used officially by any military unit. Actually Ferguson's rifle was the practical development of the same screw plug breechloader produced by La Chaumette some seventy years before. Ferguson himself claimed invention only for his improvements on La Chaumette's original idea.

EFFECTIVENESS OF THE PENNSYLVANIA RIFLE

What made the Pennsylvania rifle so effective? The answer seems to be that it was a combination of expert barrel-making skill coupled with the voiced needs of the American backwoodsman. He wanted a light rifle of simple construction which he could keep in ordinary repair; a rifle of small bore to save the powder and lead he had to pack on his back for it, as well as to keep shooting costs low; a rifle with a barrel length to burn up the complete powder charge which in those days varied in quality. With his powder charge and the size of bullet he liked best, he estimated that his gun was no gun at all if it would not shoot and be accurate at least 250 paces — like others he knew and could talk about.

Finally, the backwoodsman knew all about using patches, either of linen or thin buckskin, and the kind of grease on them which worked best in his gun. This patch, a small square piece, was wrapped around the ball with only a short skirt protruding when the ball was inserted at the muzzle. He knew how smoothly the balls with these patches should ram down the bore and what the patch could tell about fouling and fit when he found one after discharge. The patch not only cleaned the bore of powder residue when rammed down but it was elastic enough to fill the space between ball and barrel to prevent the escape of gas; and at the same time, it hugged the rifle grooves giving the spin required in firing to make the ball fly true to the mark.

The patch had been used for more than 200 years in Europe. Why was it apparently so much more effective in an American rifle? The smaller size of the ball seems to be one answer. The development of the proper twist or curve in the rifling to work best with the powder charge and weight of ball used appears to be another. Very likely also, both gunsmith and backwoodsman had learned something about the casting of good, clean, smooth balls, of even density without seams or pits. Accuracy was improved also because these American rifles of small caliber had far less recoil than their big-calibered, European predecessors, to say nothing of the longer sighting radius provided by their longer barrels.

In its performance, the Pennsylvania (Kentucky) rifle was a fine, skilled, American product — almost an institution — which pioneered in a craftmanship whose benefits are still with us. It was our first

"All-American." It not only won the East as many another later fire-arm claims the winning of the West, but, more than that, it had a large part in winning a place on this continent for a democracy called the United States of America. The balance of its story will come later.

PISTOLS

The flintlock "horse pistol" was not in common use before the Revolution because the need of the Colonial was for a hunting gun or rifle or musket for the different phases of his life — daily food, defense against Indians, or service in the militia for local frontier defense. Personal feuds were not yet currently governed or to be satis-fied by challenges under a punctilious duelling code with dignified messages handled by seconds under a strict etiquette of honor. All that came some years later, perhaps the most important episode being in 1804, of which more anon.

During the Revolution many pistols, often in pairs called a brace, were required by officers of the higher ranks. Usually they were personal property. For rank and file, some of the dragoons or cavalry as well as naval personnel required them. Most of these pistols came from Europe, being of German, Dutch, Belgian, and French origin, though a good many of English manufacture found their way into American hands by way of dealers in the Caribbean. Lafayette alone is said to have procured several hundred Charleville pistols. In addition there were a few like those by Rappahannock Forge (James Hunter), Falmouth, Virginia, which were good weapons too. But the American-made pistols were in a very small minority because the Colonial gun-smiths were more practised in making guns for which the official and private demand was continuous.

French Charleville Pistol

CHAPTER IV

FROM THE REVOLUTION TO THE END
OF THE MEXICAN WAR

The thirteen colonies, having by war and a formal peace treaty with Great Britain firmly established the United States of America, now set about the business of establishing good and sufficient magazines for reception of the public arms and munitions. These were to be established at West Point; Yellow Springs, Pennsylvania; New London, Virginia; and Springfield, Massachusetts. By 1784 the bulk of the old Continental Army had been discharged and Washington had resigned his commission.

Other crises, however, made evident that the price of peace, as well as freedom, is eternal vigilance. Soon after the war ended there were some minor internal disturbances; and the frontier, with its Indian problems, always continued to roll westward. There were arguments with England over seaboard rights and the rights of American seamen. And there were troubles with the Barbary pirates operating out of Morocco, Tripoli, and Tunis. Altogether, there were twenty years of a tribute-covered commerce until the United States sent a fleet into the harbor of Algiers and forced the end of this international banditry. In 1798 we also had some naval arguments with France. After that came the question of what, in their bartering of empires, Spain or Napoleon would do with Louisiana.

Then almost overnight a remarkable trade took place affecting the history not only of the United States but also of the world at large. Spain ceded Louisiana to France. Napoleon, badly needing money for the impending war with England, sold Louisiana outright to the United States in 1803, thus in one supreme sweep giving the United States a contested 2000-mile jump to the Pacific Ocean.

However we must go back a bit to bring the record of firearms development up to the Louisiana Purchase. Under contract with Pennsylvania gunsmiths, the government bought rifles to equip the new rifle battalion authorized in 1792.[1] In 1794 it established national

---

[1] These rifles were made by Peter Gonter, Jr., Lancaster, Pennsylvania, and others. Gonter also was one of the contractors furnishing rifles for the Government Indian trade, these being made between 1803 and 1807.

arsenals at Springfield, Massachusetts, and Harpers Ferry, Virginia. As a model for its first government-produced military gun, it selected the French Charleville musket, Model of 1763, which had proven so satisfactory in the Revolutionary War. This musket was of .69 caliber instead of the ¾-inch bore of the British Brown Bess; the barrel was fastened to the stock with bands instead of pins or keys as was the Brown Bess. The Springfield Armory was the first to produce this musket, since it had been a depot for some years whereas Harpers Ferry had to be built from the foundation. The musket is called the U. S. Model 1795. Varying with the opinions of different authorities, from four to six models of this flintlock were made with minor modifications, ending when the percussion smoothbore Model of 1842 was authorized.

TREASON, CODES OF HONOR, AND DUELS

Still vivid in the minds of the rebelling Colonials was the contrast of the treasonable conduct of Benedict Arnold and Charles Lee compared to a code of honor personified by Captain Nathan Hale and one declared in the ringing words by Patrick Henry. It was difficult to forget these episodes of the recent struggle. Thus, with personal honor and integrity so emphasized, duelling came more and more into vogue with the result that duelling pistols of fine craftsmanship, paired and in cases with all accoutrements, were not uncommon private possessions. Since one duel already had been fought regarding Washington's leadership of the army (Cadwalader-Conway), no doubt duelling was also partly an inheritance from associations with European elite in the recent war. Yet pistols, it may be said, were not the only dueling weapons. The challenged party had the right to choose the weapons to be used. Some of the choices were: sword, saber, bowie knife, rifle, shot gun, or club. Two examples of duels, famous in their time, are given below.

THE BURR-HAMILTON DUEL, 1804. — Colonel Aaron Burr, named in 1801 as Jefferson's vice-president, was an unscrupulous politician. Alexander Hamilton for some years had an unfavorable opinion of Burr and had not hesitated in voicing his opinions. Burr knew this but had made no complaints. While still Vice-President, Burr in a bitter contest endeavored to secure election as Governor of New York State. During this campaign, Hamilton made some disparaging remarks about Burr. In chagrin at his political defeat, Burr voiced offense and challenged Hamilton to a duel. They met at Weehawken, New Jersey, in July, 1804, on the same spot where, a short time before, Hamilton's son had been killed in a so-called "affair of honor." Only one shot was exchanged and Hamilton, who had fired in the air, fell mortally wounded. But this duel ruined completely the further public life of Aaron Burr. The next year he was conniving to set up an independent government in Louisiana and southwest into Spanish territory. His friend General James Wilkinson, who testified against Burr to save his own position as department commander, was found later to have been in the pay of the Spanish. These developments sustained Hamilton's judgment about Burr and added to the sorrowful portrait of ambitious men who might have been brilliant figures in history had they been true.

THE JACKSON-DICKINSON DUEL, 1806. — From boyhood in the Revolutionary War where he was wounded in the minor conflicts of the Carolina backwoods, Andrew Jackson had been a fighter, a loyal friend, and a bitter enemy. As a grown man he was quick to protect his personal honor and that of his family. As a young lawyer in 1788, he had a duel with Colonel Waightstill Avery, a scholarly old attorney, based on a case in court in which Jackson alleged that Avery had taken fees illegally. By sunset of the following day, the contestants met on a hill outside the town of Jonesboro. In the meantime, conciliators had accomplished their work so that both parties fired in the air and soon shook hands.

But Jackson's second duel in 1806 was neither so transitory nor so harmless. It started with the garbled story of payments for horse-racing bets being made to Jackson with promissory notes by Charles Dickinson and his horse racing friend Captain Joseph Erwin. The story finally involved several men, two at least engaging in a separate duel in which one suffered a wound in the thigh. In this general squabble, Jackson's real ferment probably started from drunken remarks made by Dickinson (for which he apologized when confronted) regarding Rachel Donelson's divorce before becoming Jackson's wife. Meanwhile Dickinson visited New Orleans and returned in time for the April 3rd "most interesting horse race ever run in the Western country between General Jackson's horse TRUXTON and Captain Joseph Erwin's horse PLOUGHBOY", as proclaimed by the advertising. Two days before the event, from hard training, Truxton had a swelling in the thigh; and Erwin and Dickinson were confident that Jackson would have to pay the forfeit. But Jackson checked his horse carefully and, in spite of the feeling of his advisors, decided to run him. He won. And the stakes earned for his partisans by Truxton were said to have been $10,000.

The loss of this horse race weighed more on the socially favored Dickinson than on anyone else. The following month, he attacked Jackson in a Nashville paper and Jackson challenged. Dickinson was a "crack shot." Firing, apparently without aim at the word of command at twenty-four feet, he could put four balls in a mark with each shot-hole touching another. In Nashville it was said that he wagered he would kill Jackson at the first fire.

But the devil himself could not subdue the indomitable will of Andrew Jackson. He was not intending to get off a quick and perhaps poorly aimed shot. So the parties met on the "field of honah." The nine-inch barrels of the duelling pistols were then loaded by the seconds — ounce balls of .70 caliber. The regulation distance of twenty-four feet was paced off and marks set. The principals took their places on the marks. Jackson wore a dark blue frock coat and trousers, fitting his thin frame loosely. The two men were signalled to be ready. Then came the word "Fire!" Almost instantly Dickinson's shot was off and a fleck of dust came from Jackson's coat. His left hand clutched his chest as he fought for self-control. Slowly he raised the pistol.

Dickinson recoiled and cried out in disbelief that he had missed. As Dickinson came back to the mark, arms folded, Jackson straightened and pulled the trigger. The pistol merely clicked as the hammer stopped at half-cock, perhaps due to Jackson's pull being weak. But calmly he again cocked the pistol, aimed, and fired. Dickinson sank to the ground.

When Jackson reached his horse, his companion noticed that his left boot was soaked with blood. Jackson said he knew he was hit but did not want the Dickinson party to know. The surgeon found that Dickinson's aim had been perfectly true, but he had misjudged Jackson's position by the fit of his coat over his unusually slender figure. But Jackson said that even if Dickinson had shot him through the brain he, Jackson, would have returned the shot.

FIRST MODEL HARPERS FERRY RIFLE, 1803

In 1799, with threats of war with France hovering, Congress authorized a rifle regiment to be added to the army. This resulted in the first official U. S. rifle, since called Model 1803 (also 1804), made at Harpers Ferry. This rifle was a composite of the Pennsylvania rifle, the heavy French military carbine, and the small German military rifle of the type confiscated after the Battle of Bennington by colonial New England troops. Four thousand of them reportedly were fabricated. They were of .54 caliber, having an overall length of 48 inches with 32¾-inch barrels. One of the authentic remaining specimens is in the West Point Museum.

It has been stated repeatedly that Harpers Ferry records were burned in early Civil War fighting there and therefore it is not known what kind, type, or number of firearms were made after the armory was ready to operate. However some competent authorities have said that there still is a mass of Harpers Ferry records awaiting the researcher. A recent National Parks Service publication on Harpers Ferry states that the gun factory was in production before the end of 1796.[2] And gunlocks of Harpers Ferry brand have been found with dates of 1800, which gives some basis for the statements of Sawyer and Bannerman that rifles were made there, perhaps experimental, about that time. Joseph Perkin, an English Moravian, had been appointed superintendent in 1796.[3]

The Harpers Ferry rifle used by the Lewis and Clark Expedition was very similar to the Model of 1803, probably a prototype because Meriwether Lewis checked his equipment there, including the rifles, in April of that year — five weeks before Henry Dearborn, Secretary

---

[2]U. S. National Parks Service, *Harpers Ferry National Monument* (Washington, D.C., 1961).

[3]The Harpers Ferry Armory, under skilled Joseph Perkin, apparently was the government research laboratory of those days. The first government-made rifle originated there and, following the fine lines of this rifle, the first government-designed pistol was made there; so was the first official breechloader. Except for halfstock and barrel length, the Model 1803 rifle was similar to the Gonter contract rifle of 1792 (as shown by Plate 11 of Colonel Berkeley R. Lewis' *Small Arms and Ammunition . . .* , Washington, D.C., Smithsonian Institution, 1956). No government-made guns were dated before 1799 and some records of the Harpers Ferry Armory were burned early in the Civil War. Therefore it is risky to be very positive about the early products of the Armory. In 1949, in Venezuela, Colonel Lewis found a Harpers Ferry blunderbuss dated 1814. Another one, stamped Harpers Ferry, 1810, with U. S. Navy marks, is in the Milwaukee Public Museum. There is little knowledge today about these pieces or reasons or authority for their origin. Furthermore as to background for origins, in reading Henry Dearborn's letter of May 25, 1803, to Joseph Perkin (cf. James E. Hicks, *Notes on United States Ordnance*, Mount Vernon, N. Y., c1940, vol. 1) one may well wonder just what was that short rifle with which Dearborn appears to be so familiar and which he mentally used to make his comparisons.

of War, authorized making 2000 rifles of the Model 1803 which were made without bayonets. Lewis had been secretary to Thomas Jefferson for two years; and Jefferson had in mind an exploring expedition to the Pacific long before the Louisiana Purchase.[4] Anyway, these rifles Lewis was checking were closely related to the Pennsylvania (Kentucky) rifle. Since by 1806 they reached the Pacific coast with Lewis and Clark, perhaps that registers another "first" for the All-American rifle.

Earlier in this book the statement was made that the Pennsylvania rifle "won the East" and the claim looks reasonable. But because attention has just been drawn to the fact that one of its descendants was the first American rifle to reach the Pacific as an adjunct of the first United States overland exploring party, there is no intention to imply that this particular rifle family also won the West. The rifle certainly played its part with Lewis and Clark as it did later in other western episodes of that great drama. But it took a long time to win the West, perhaps seventy years from the event referred to above.

OTHER HARPERS FERRY EARLY PRODUCTS[5]

MODEL 1805 PISTOL. — The first government-made pistol was the Harpers Ferry Model 1805, a flintlock in caliber .54. This pistol bears strong resemblance to the fine lines of the Model 1803 Harpers Ferry rifle. Various other martial flintlock pistols were made by Springfield Armory, Simeon North, Asa Waters, J. J. Henry, Henry Aston, R. & J. D. Johnson, and others. The Johnson pistol, made in 1844, was the final one of the flintlock martials many of which were soon to be converted to the next step in the ignition system, the percussion caplock, which will be considered presently.

THE HALL BREECHLOADER. — After several years of testing and trial, partly at Harpers Ferry, a new type of flintlock breechloader was undertaken in 1819. This rifled gun was invented by John H. Hall and William Thornton, Hall's first patent being issued in 1811. After a few test rifles had been made under contract and proved satisfactory, Hall was engaged to go to Harpers Ferry to further perfect

---

[4]Meriwether Lewis, *Original Journals of the Lewis and Clark Expedition,* 1804-1806. Edited, with introduction, notes, and index, by Reuben Gold Thwaites (New York, 1905), v. 1, pp. xx-xxii.
[5]Refer to footnote 3 at bottom of page 29.

the arm which was to be made with fully interchangeable parts — a French idea. Now for the first time this was to be done in a United States armory though previously it had been done by gun contractors Eli Whitney and Simeon North. A separate plant was built in due course at Harpers Ferry for the Hall products which included smooth-bores both in long guns and carbines for the use of cartridges using a combination of one lead ball and three buckshot, commonly called "buck and ball", but in calibers larger than the rifle .52. When the first of the regulation .52 caliber breechloaders was issued to troops, the United States became the first nation in the world to officially adopt such a firearm.[6]

1815: WITHOUT THE RIFLE PERSONALLY DEMONSTRATED, NAPOLEON WOULD NOT BELIEVE

While inventor Hall was working on his breech-loading models in Portland, Maine, the continuing difficulties with England expanded into the War of 1812. This conflict was peculiar because, both at the beginning and the end, events were ahead of what facts would have prevented. Means of communication then were dreadfully slow. At the beginning, Congress declared war before being aware of the concessions made by England. At the end, Andrew Jackson fought and won the Battle of New Orleans two weeks after the peace treaty had been signed.

Jackson had about 4000 men: 500 regulars armed with muskets; 500 regulars armed with the Harpers Ferry Model 1803 rifle; volunteer riflemen from Kentucky, Tennessee, and Louisiana — about 2100 in all — self-armed and self-equipped with hunting rifles; and, finally, several hundred pirates under Jean LaFitte who handled the artillery. The British force, under General Sir Edward Pakenham, was composed mainly of 7500 veterans who had served under Wellington in Spain and were considered the finest infantry in the world. But the accurate work of the long, American hunting rifle in the hands of some of

---

[6]The British Ferguson flintlock breechloader, used in the Revolutionary War, was the first breech-loading shoulder arm used officially by any military force, but it was not an officially adopted weapon as was the Hall. The breech-loading idea was not new; it had been a matter of experiment for over 200 years.

America's keenest sharpshooters, coupled with the Harpers Ferry rifle, backed by solid support from muskets and cleverly handled artillery, far outclassed the British smoothbores levelled with the regulation volley fire. General Pakenham was killed; his second in command General Gibbs died from wounds; and General Keene who next took command was severely wounded. There were nearly 2500 casualties among the British infantry. Jackson's men had less than 100 hit. Afterward, General Jackson said, "I never had so grand and awful an idea of a resurrection . . . (when) I saw . . . more than five hundred Britons emerging from heaps of their dead comrades, all over the plain rising up, and . . . coming forward . . . as prisoners."[7]

Having read Latour and other primary accounts, Rowland stated:

> After the terrible battle that had lasted scarcely more than an hour, the dead, the dying and the wounded could be traced in a long scarlet strip over the plains, and along the levees and bayous, a writhing, disfigured mass that filled the beholder with horror and dismay. Beyond, the great dark forest outlined the river; the long Spanish moss, bedraggled by wind and rain, shrouding the bare limbs of trees, lent an added touch of dreariness to the heart-rending scene.[8]

As Sawyer summarized, the Battle of New Orleans was the first major engagement between the smoothbore and the rifle. Europe was amazed. In exile Napoleon refused to believe the report unless he could see the arms fired.

THE PERCUSSION LOCK, 1817

Two years after Jackson's victory at New Orleans, with thin copper punched into a capsule, Joshua Shaw was perfecting his percussion cap which replaced the flintlock method of firing. By 1825, the new percussion system was making good headway in commercial gunmaking.

[7]Marquis James, *Andrew Jackson, the Border Captain* (Indianapolis, 1930), p. 267. See also William Garrott Brown, *Andrew Jackson* (Boston, 1900), pp. 79-80, from which the quotation as originally given was taken. Word in parentheses added by author.
[8]Eron Rowland, *Andrew Jackson's Campaign Against the British . . . War of 1812* (New York, 1926), p. 358. (Copyright by Eron Rowland, 1926; The Macmillan Co., New York, 1926)

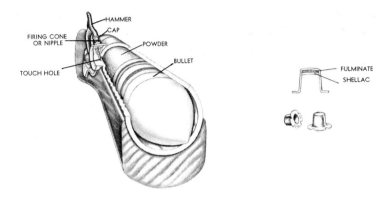

HAMMER

CAP

FIRING CONE
OR NIPPLE

POWDER

BULLET

TOUCH HOLE

FULMINATE

SHELLAC

Percussion Lock and Copper Caps

The copper percussion cap contained an explosive fulminate detonated by a blow from what was now to be called a "hammer" instead of the cock. The idea of percussion ignition was originated in 1807 by Alexander Forsyth, a Scottish minister, who first used the fulminate powder in suitable receptacles and later with the powder formed into pellets for easy handling. But it remained for Shaw to make the idea more practical by sticking a bit of the powder in the base of his copper cap, covered with thin foil and waterproofed with shellac or similar adhesive. This copper cup, the cap, was placed over a hollow steel firing cone or nipple which it hugged firmly; and the cone was threaded to a hollow receptacle leading directly to the powder charge in the barrel. The tiny bit of fulminate responded violently to a sharp blow sending a quantity of burning gas under considerable pressure into the powder-charged gun chamber. But as will be seen below, sixteen years elapsed before the United States issued to troops guns with the percussion system. Even as late as the Mexican War, 1846-47, General Winfield Scott preferred the flintlock because it was a tried and proven weapon in military service generally.

In 1833, under Hall's breech-loading patent heretofore mentioned, Simeon North, Middletown, Connecticut, made expressly for the United States Dragoons, a newly organized mounted regiment, the first percussion, breech-loading arm in government service. Major Richard B. Mason of the Dragoons was responsible for these carbines being made smoothbore in .69 caliber so that they would shoot buckshot as well as ball cartridge. The actual diameter of the ball inside its paper capsule was about .64.

Hall Breechloading Carbine, Patent 1846 (made by S. North)

All other shoulder arms, until 1841, continued to be made as flintlocks, the last pistol flintlock being made in 1844 as previously stated. After that year for newly made arms of all types, long or short, the percussion system was current. And from the end of the Mexican War, especially from 1848, thousands of flintlocks were altered at government arsenals and by commercial shops to use the percussion cap.

Between 1825 and 1830, the percussion system had become general in commercial gunmaking. Production of the Pennsylvania type rifle had spread over most of the area from New England to the Carolinas and some of these gunmakers already had settled in St. Louis following the migration of settlers into Kentucky and the river traffic into the Mississippi.

THE FAMOUS HAWKEN RIFLE

The story of the Hawken rifle ranges wide not only in area but also in elapsed time. It was made principally as a percussion gun and was the favorite of fur trappers and traders, the mountain men of the 1825-1850 period. At the annual trader rendezvous in the Rockies, it was passed from hand to hand until most of these men of the wilds had one. Some of the prominent owners were Kit Carson, Jim Bridger,

James Clyman, William H. Ashley, and Edwin T. Denig of the American Fur Company.

Hawken Rifle

In the beginning there were three Hawkins (or Hawkens), the father Henry and two sons Jacob and Samuel. Henry Hawkins had a gunshop in Lancaster, Pennsylvania, about 1800. Then he worked in the Harpers Ferry Armory and later set up his own shop at Hagerstown, Maryland. But the western trail was calling Henry. So he made his way across Kentucky and, with his son Jacob then 22 years old, arrived in St. Louis in 1808. At first they may have worked for LeConte, a gunsmith who was active in St. Louis before 1804. However that may be, the Hawkins were there early enough to have heard first-hand stories of the men returning from the Lewis and Clark Expedition and probably all about the Harpers Ferry rifle. But probably they already knew more about it than anyone in St. Louis except as to its performance on its round trip to the Pacific.

Jacob Hawkins opened his own shop in 1815 and made rifles with some similarity to the Pennsylvania except they were shorter, more like the Harpers Ferry. These of course were flintlocks and so few in number that none appear to have survived. Other gunmakers followed the Hawkins: J. V. Bouis came before 1819, Louis Magueron arrived between 1819 and 1821, and James Lakenan appeared in 1821.

In 1820 Henry Hawkins died and two years later Jacob's younger brother Samuel joined him. That same year they set up shop on the levee, changing the family name, for some unknown reason, to Hawken.

At that time St. Louis was well on its way as the big-river, commercial center above New Orleans. It was soon to be the headquarters of the fur business with the office of the American Fur Company located there. So it not only catered to the fur trapper and trader, but also being midway between tall timber and the high plains, it would soon be transshipping supplies for the trade to the west and southwest, the goods being delivered to traders at Independence and Westport Landing (Kansas City). Westport was the starting point for most of those western venturers who, using the saddle, needed rifles suited for the mountains and the plains. The mountain man came first, so his rifle was called the Mountain Rifle. Years later, when the plains carried Texas Rangers, Santa Fe traders, buffalo hunters, and cattle, the gun was called the Plains Rifle.

Meanwhile, for their trade, these early St. Louis gunsmiths relied upon the river traffic, the settlers in the adjacent country, and their expectations of exploration and other travel westward. The Hawken brothers made a plain, serviceable and accurate rifle. Others may have excelled in some of the niceties of workmanship but none did better in meeting the practical needs of the fur trapper, trader, and plainsman. The partnership of J. & S. Hawken was located at 214 North Main Street until 1832 when it moved to 33 Washington Avenue where it had over thirty gunsmiths working for it. Jacob died in 1849. In 1862, Samuel T. Hawken sold the business to one of his gunsmiths, John P. Gemmer, who carried on the work under the Hawken name. At that time, the Hawkens had been making percussion rifles thirty years or more.

John P. Gemmer lived until 1919. In his lifetime he had seen the end of the great fur trade to the Rockies and the long caravans to the Southwest over the Santa Fe Trail. He had seen the advent of the metallic cartridge, as best marked by the Civil War, and with that the slow fadeout of the percussion rifle.[9]

---

[9]John P. Gemmer left a son, John P. H. Gemmer, who later had great interest in guns. This man assembled an impressive collection of the early gunmaker's art, and part of it may be seen today in the Jefferson Memorial Building of the Missouri Historical Society in St. Louis.

Not until 1849 did another gunmaker establish a name of comparable reputation to Hawken in St. Louis and the vast outland beyond; and by that time the West was changing. This gunmaker was Horace E. Dimick who not only made good guns and some pistols, but also was a dealer in firearms made in the East. Dimick finally was employing 26 gunsmiths. He died in 1874.

IMPORTANCE OF THE PERCUSSION CAP

The invention of the percussion cap was a basic new step in fire-arm progress. The advantage of the percussion cap was not alone in its simplicity, certainty of ignition, and resistance to wetting. In addition, for the multi-fire weapons such as the pistols with two, three, and four or more barrels and the rifles with two barrels, all barrels could be capped in advance ready for action.

Multi-barreled pistols, with early ignition systems and guns loading from magazines under the same risky forms of ignition, had been produced individually for hundreds of years, but none was cheap or easy to make and exceedingly few were practical. Revolvers also had been made in small numbers such as the Collier (perhaps conceived by Artemus Wheeler and others) using flint ignition but with the same drawback of high cost. Bear well in mind that some of these Collier revolvers had been sold to British forces in India.

Now the percussion cap was to open an entirely new phase in fire-arm invention. The first real step in this came in 1836 when a young man of twenty-two commercially produced the first practical revolving firearm. This was a percussion five-shot revolver which, by cocking the hammer, automatically turned the cylinder, aligned each succeeding chamber with the bore of the barrel, and locked it in place for firing. The name of this youthful inventor was Samuel Colt of Hartford, Connecticut. This revolver had both practicality and simplicity permitting a reasonable cost to the purchaser. The difficulty was to demonstrate its advantages. It might be ahead of its time.

Collier Flintlock Revolver

SAMUEL COLT'S REVOLVING FIREARMS, 1836

The intriguing story of Samuel Colt has had much attention. There were only twenty-six years left for this young man to live, but he put every year to intensive effort. What of his earlier life?

At an early age he found much interest in a book which told of inventions — particularly of a galvanic battery and the making of gunpowder. From this reading and consequent stimulation of ideas, he started experimenting, eventually finding out how to waterproof insulated wire to explode a powder charge under water, and finally to blow a raft "sky high." His grandfather, Major John Caldwell who was a veteran of the Revolutionary War, gave the boy a horse pistol and thrilled him with tales of men who had marched with Washington. The favorite story was about Tim Murphy and his double-barreled rifle.[10] Sam tried to exceed these exploits by fastening together four barrels to revolve about a central axis and be fired with one lock, but the contrivance blew up.

Sam was the son of a manufacturer of cloth goods. His mother died in 1821 when he was seven. In 1823 his father Christopher Colt married Olive Sargeant. At age ten, Sam was sent to his father's factory at Ware, Massachusetts, where he remained until he was sent to school at Amherst.

When he was about sixteen years old, his father arranged to send him to sea. Before the ship was ready to sail, Sam got involved indirectly at Amherst in a rather damaging Fourth of July celebration with gunpowder which caused a severe reaction by the school authorities. As a result, Sam left school and arrived home unexpectedly. However soon after, on August 2, 1830, he sailed from Boston for Calcutta on the ship Corlo, Captain Spaulding, as a seaman before the mast.[11]

---

[10]This Tim Murphy was of Colonel Daniel Morgan's command while confronting Burgoyne at Saratoga. Murphy, an expert rifleman, was asked to shoot Brigadier General Simon Fraser who was a host in himself as a fighting British leader. At a very considerable distance, from a tree Murphy fired three shots, the last one passing through Fraser's body, thus taking the punch out of Burgoyne's shock troops and providing another cause for his surrender. The Pennsylvania rifle again!

[11]Henry Barnard, ed., *Armsmear, the House, the Arm and the Armory of Samuel Colt. A Memorial.* (New York, 1866). Found among his papers after Sam's death in 1862, were several old letters. One dated August 2, 1830, was by Samuel Lawrence of the mercantile firm of Lawrence, Stone & Company, Boston, to Sam's father enclosing the bill for $91.24 covering Sam's outfit as a sailor. Wrote Lawrence: "The ship sailed this morning. The last time I saw Sam, he was . . . on the fore-topsail yard, loosing the top sail . . . He is a manly fellow." To enable the boy to bring home something from the far east, Mr. Lawrence "told the super-cargo to advance him $50.00 if he required."

Enroute to India he worked out the plan of a separate cylinder chambered for five charges of ball and powder rotating behind a single barrel. Thus he improved his idea of using a cluster of full-length barrels as he tried to do from the stories of Tim Murphy's double gun. For holding each successive chamber in line with the barrel, he noted how the upright spoke of the ship's steering wheel (some say the capstan) was always indexed at the same point by a latching device. With these ideas gained, he whittled out the first model of the revolver.

One must remember that Sam was a born salesman and so judge these tales, which must have originated with him, as being influenced by the promotion of his revolver. Thus some infer that actually when the ship reached India, Sam saw the Collier revolver in the hands of British officers and was allowed to examine it thoroughly. But it is quite as likely that Colt saw the revolving-cylinder rifle made by William Billinghurst of Rochester, New York, in the early 1830's. Anyway, Sam Colt, a boy without money, certainly had initiative.

After his year's voyage he returned to the factory, and, from the bleaching and dyeing foreman, learned something about chemistry. While engaged with this, he made, with the help of a gunsmith, two models of his revolver but both were unworkable. However, with the new knowledge he had gained from the chemical foreman, at the age of eighteen he assumed the pseudonym of "Dr. Coult of New York, London, and Calcutta", and thus, as a savant of some authority, travelled over the country giving lectures and demonstrations with nitrous oxide or "laughing gas." He must have pleased his audiences because he not only made his expense money but also enough to finance the making of better models by a good gunmaker, John Pearson of Baltimore. Some of these Pearson models are to be seen now in the Wadsworth Atheneum, Hartford, Connecticut.

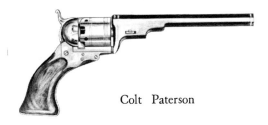

Colt Paterson

With these working models he obtained patents in the United States, France, and England. In 1836, he formed the Patent Arms Manufacturing Company at Paterson, New Jersey, and commenced making five-shot revolvers and revolving long guns, some with eight-shot cylinders. A number of his rifles sold to the government were used in the Seminole War. But these weapons using the new percussion cap were a little ahead of their time.

SAM'S "PEPPERBOX" COMPETITORS

About this time there commenced to appear on the market multi-barreled, percussion, revolving pistols of four or more chambers, later given the nickname "Pepperbox." These were made by Allen; Allen, Thurber & Co.; Allen & Wheelock; Darling; Stocking; and others, including later, several from Europe. In all these pepperboxes, the charges were loaded at the muzzles of the clustered barrels instead of from the front of the cylinder as on Colt's revolver; and so their construction made them considerably cheaper.

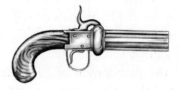

Pepperbox, This Model Having Been Made by J. Englehart
for B. and B. M. Darling

The average pepperbox, a pocket piece, was not much of a lethal weapon. It was inaccurate because of its flopping "mule ear" hammer directly in the line of sight actuated by a double-action trigger. But its rapid fire at close quarters was intimidating and it was fairly cheap. So thousands of them were carried by people travelling over the western trails — settlers, miners, hunters, traders, and adventurers.

Consequently, with sales limited and no profit, about 1842 the creditors forced Colt out of business, and in 1845 it was completely liquidated. So Colt went back to his early experiments with the galvanic battery, waterproofed wires, and underwater explosions. In this work, explained as being valuable for harbor defense, he interested members of Congress sufficiently to get an appropriation of $20,000 to continue his experiments.

THE FIRST ARMY REVOLVER, 1847

About this time the Mexican War threatened and United States troops under Zachary Taylor were sent to Texas. Among the Texas Rangers hoping to join Taylor in case of actual war, came Samuel Walker who had served in the war against the Seminole Indians, under Lieutenant Colonel William S. Harney in whose command Colt's revolvers and rifles had been used. After war was declared, Walker was made a captain in the new regiment of Mounted Rifles. He was sent to his home area at Baltimore on recruiting duty. He met Sam Colt and coached by Sam, with the help of the President and the Secretary of War, he was soon endeavoring to get Colt revolvers for his new regiment. The result was the first official army revolver, the Colt-Walker, of which 1100 were made by Eli Whitney, Jr. One thousand were for the army and 100 for disposition otherwise — mainly as gifts or promotional advertising. This was a very large and heavy weapon. It weighed 4 lbs. 9 oz. and had a nine-inch barrel. Its .44 caliber required conical balls running 32 to the pound or round balls of 48 to the pound. So the conical balls weighed about ½ oz. each. With fifty grains of black powder, this was almost a load fit for a rifle. The full story of the revolver and its history in the Mexican War is told in *Frontier Steel* published for the Eastern Washington State Historical Society.

First Army Revolver, the Colt-Walker

PERCUSSION LOCKS IN THE MEXICAN WAR, 1846-47

As a general statement one might say that the Mexican War was fought with flintlocks. The outstanding exception was the regiment of Mississippians commanded by Jefferson Davis. The Colt-Walker revolver, of course, was another exception, but actually only 500 of them reached Mexico and their use was limited to guerrilla fighting after Mexico City had been captured and the Mexican army dispersed. Also in this war some pepperboxes were used.

MODEL 1841 HARPERS FERRY OR "MISSISSIPPI RIFLE". — In 1841, Harpers Ferry Armory produced the first U. S. Army regulation, muzzle-loading percussion rifle. This rifle was of .54 caliber with a 33-inch barrel. It was patterned after the Model 1803 and the Model 1814, the butt stock being shaped like the latter, with full forestock having one plain rear band and a front band with double loops on top, an integral ramrod throat, and a sling swivel of iron on the under side. The trigger guard was plain with swivel in front and the patch box was quite similar to the Model 1803, being made, like the other fittings, of brass. A few hundred of the rifles were made at the Springfield Armory but most of them were supplied under contract by commercial firms such as Eli Whitney, New Haven, Connecticut; Robbins and Lawrence, Windsor, Vermont; E. Remington, Ilion, New York; and Edward K. Tryon, Philadelphia. In large measure, those made by the above firms were issued to the militia of various states. Combining government and contract production, about 10,000 of these rifles were made. During its twenty-five years of military service, the rifle acquired more names than any other, being called: "Jaeger" or "Yager", "Mississippi rifle", "Mississippi Yager or Yerger", and finally in the Civil War "Kentucky rifle." However, it became famous first in the Mexican War as the Mississippi rifle because of its impressive use by the Mississippi regiment of infantry commanded by Jefferson Davis.

U. S. Model 1841 Rifle

The Harpers Ferry 1841 rifle was noteworthy for being the best made and most accurate spherical bullet rifle in the world. It so remained until the adoption of the conical Minie' bullet in 1855 when a new model was devised to use this conical bullet. The powder charge for the half-ounce, Model 1841, spherical ball was 75 grains of rifle powder. The muzzle velocity was about 1850 feet per second. Cartridges for it were made with the ball patched and tallowed, and placed in the paper cylinder over the powder with the patch pucker to the front. Over this the paper cylinder was drawn together and tied with three turns and a double hitch of linen thread. In loading, the folded end of the paper cylinder next to the powder was torn off, usually with the teeth; the powder poured into the barrel followed by the patched ball; and the paper capsule thrown away.[12]

NEW HORIZONS WESTWARD

The racing twelve-year stretch from 1836 to 1848 was a portentous period for the United States on its trail toward "Manifest Destiny." To start it, there was the epic struggle at the Alamo in San Antonio leading to the union of the Republic of Texas with the United States nearly ten years later. The acquisition of the Colt revolver by the Texas Rangers a few years after the Alamo massacre upset the supremacy of the Comanche Indians (and eventually the Cheyenne, Sioux, and other tribes of the plains) as the "finest cavalry in the world." The Mexican War settled the boundary of Texas at the Rio Grande. With the marches to the Pacific via New Mexico and Arizona by Kearny with his escort of two companies of the First U. S. Dragoons, and by Cooke with the Mormon Battalion, added to the activities of the U. S. Navy and Fremont in California, that great uncemented province of Mexico became part of the United States. Also in 1847 over the central route west, there transpired the epochal migration of the Mormons to the Great Salt Lake Basin. Meanwhile we had settled the question of Oregon Territory — "54-40 or Fight" — with England

---

[12]For Civil War use, most of the Model 1841 rifles were altered to use the regulation .58 caliber Minie' ball; and lugs for saber bayonets were added near the muzzle. Several Zouave regiments were armed with these rifles. Remington made a so-called "Zouave rifle" with rectangular patch box, two bands and plain fore end, quite similar to the Model 1855 rifle except it did not have the Maynard tape primer. The 1855 Model rifle-musket was a longer piece than the Model 1855 rifle and it had no patch box.

by a peaceful agreement. And our pioneer settlers, following the fur trappers and traders in an ever widening stream, were pouring into the great west by the thousands.

BUT NARROWED HORIZONS FOR THE INDIAN

Now for the moment, to get a broader view of what effect this was having and would have on the Indian, expand the vision a generation each way from the end of the Mexican War. First take a look backward. From about 1820 the fur trappers and traders, the mountain men, had steadily increased in numbers and trade volume. The Texas Ranger with his newly acquired Colt revolver was only another straw in the wind of the plains. Following fast after the vanguard, explorers, settlers, missionaries, and gold seekers took the western trails, killing enroute the game, especially the buffalo on which the Indian depended for his existence.

Now look ahead to the 1860's when the Union Pacific Railroad was being built. Sharps rifles had been killing buffalo on the plains for a decade. With later improvements in drawing out or lengthening the brass cartridge case for more powder, thus increasing the power and the range of the rifle, the slaughter of the buffalo went on at a great rate. This consumed the Indian's means of livelihood while filling the effete East with buffalo robes for winter sleighing as well as providing buffalo coats for any place where the going was bitter. At the same time, industry took even more for sole leather and belting.

As a consequence of the pressures outlined above, during one generation after the Mexican War, the Indians, in tribes often at war with each other, joined in a common front to resist this white invasion. By 1880, the Indians were beaten in battle, their old hunting grounds were taken away, and they were forced to live on reservations.

Late Hudson's Bay Trade Gun

SERPENTINE SIDEPLATE

In Canada, unlike the United States, the pioneer settler did not follow on the heels of the trapper and trader. So in Canada, carrying the Hudson's Bay trade gun, from the time of the American Revolution, the Indian hunted and trapped for one hundred years with little interference and trouble; and the Hudson's Bay Company (and other traders as could manage elsewhere or around the chartered border) bought from the Indian all the furs he could supply.

CHAPTER V

FROM THE CLOSE OF THE MEXICAN WAR TO THE END OF THE PERCUSSION ERA, 1865

The development of new primers and cartridges naturally presaged the development of new firearms. The Mexican War and the Civil War both stimulated these developments. Inventions rapidly followed one after another, often interlocking and sometimes opening several new avenues at once. This chapter, therefore, will describe the change in cartridges from fabric containers plus caps to the final self-primed metallic form; at the same time, and step by step, paralleling these changes as closely as possible with the resulting changes in the firearms themselves.

PAPER CARTRIDGES AND CAPS

When in 1833 Simeon North arranged to make the Hall breech-loading percussion carbines for the new regiment of U. S. Dragoons, the copper percussion caps for these carbines had to be procured from commercial shops because the government neither made nor stocked them. This situation persisted even after Harpers Ferry and other gun shops were producing the U. S. Model 1841 (Mississippi) percussion rifle, and it was not changed until after 1845. The muzzle-loading cartridge for several hundred years had been made of paper, cloth, foil, or other material. All fabric-covered cartridges were rather fragile. For the military man, cartridges (i.e. powder and ball wrapped inside a fabric capsule) were carried in compartmented boxes to keep them intact and dry. Also a small fleece-lined leather box on the soldier's belt held the percussion caps for them. Revolver cartridges were the most fragile because, being much smaller than those for guns and having to be smooth for proper loading, they employed a membrane or thin onion skin fabric glued to the ball. This fabric, because of chemical treatment to make it ignite instantly, often became brittle enough to crack in handling, thus losing powder. So these cartridges were supplied in shellacked, waterproof packets containing five or six cartridges as required.

PIN-FIRE AND FLOBERT CARTRIDGES

The fast moving shift to the new percussion cap only presaged another and more drastic change. The start of this important and far reaching development took place in Europe about the time Sam Colt produced his first Paterson revolvers. It was a completely self-contained cartridge with a metal case in which the ignition was caused by placing a bit of Forsyth's percussion powder in a tiny cup (reminiscent of Joshua Shaw) *inside* the cartridge case, with one end of a stout blunt pin resting on it, the other end sticking out of the side of the base of the cartridge to be struck by the hammer of the weapon. This invention, by the Frenchman Lefaucheux, was called a "pin-fire" cartridge, obviously to be loaded from the rear or breech of the weapon because the pin of the cartridge had to protrude through a vertical slot for the blow of the hammer. As an improvement on this ignition, about the start of the Mexican War, Flobert another Frenchman succeeded in perfecting a rim-fire cartridge with the percussion powder inside the rim like the .22 caliber "B-B" cartridge shown below.[1] But his cartridge contained only percussion fulminate which also acted as the propellant.

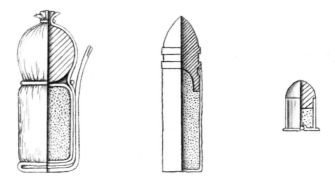

Cartridges: Paper and Linen and "B-B" Cartridge

[1]The B-B cartridge is the more common term for the Bullet Breech cap.

NEW TYPE REVOLVERS AND BREECHLOADERS

Mid century was at hand and mechanics everywhere in the United States were either altering or preparing to alter flintlocks to percussion ignition. Inventions of newer types of firearms were already in view, with the full import of the combined work of Forsyth, Shaw, and Flobert contained in a single metallic shell coming into practical focus in the Civil War when rim-fire cartridges in all common calibers up to .58 were to be used.

In 1848, Colt was making a smaller type of his first army revolver. This smaller weapon he named the Dragoon. Like the Colt-Walker, it was a .44 caliber but its cylinder was shorter and the barrel from one to one and one-half inches less in length leaving the piece about one-half pound lighter. In 1849-1850, Colt was making small pocket models in .31 and .36 caliber with short barrels — one called the "Baby Dragoon" and another similar one the "Wells Fargo." In 1851, he brought out a "Navy" model in .36 caliber, of about the same length as the Dragoon but about one and one-half pounds lighter. Two years later he produced a similar type but with a fluted cylinder as a pocket model. The heavy four-pound Dragoon was made until the Civil War and several of the other models until about 1870.

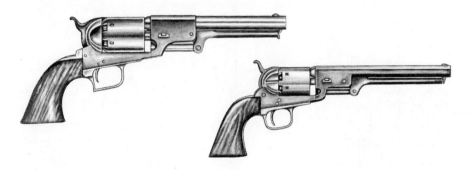

Colt Dragoon Revolver, Model 1848; and Colt Navy Revolver, Model 1851

Christian Sharps obtained two patents, 1848 and 1852, for a new breech-loading percussion gun with a downward sliding block operated by underlever. This used not only caps of the regulation percussion type but also a flat copper disc primer which automatically fed from a magazine in the lockplate near the hammer. The closing breechblock, as it rose, cut off the rear tip of the linen cartridge, thus exposing the powder. And being tighter, by means of a copper ring in the face of the breechblock and a bushed chamber which combined with the ring to restrict gas leakage, it eventually displaced the Hall which the First Dragoons had used for sixteen years from the period of their organization in 1833-34.

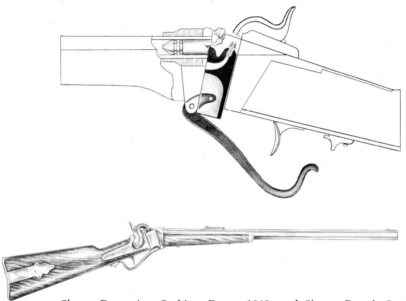

Sharps Percussion Carbine, Patent 1848; and Sharps Breech System

IMPROVED FLOBERT — THE FIRST REAL SELF-CONTAINED, RIM-FIRE CARTRIDGE

Shortly after 1854, Horace Smith and Daniel B. Wesson, inventive gunmakers of experience in the United States, developed the Flobert B-B into what became the ordinary .22 short. They used, of course, black powder as the propellant; Flobert's rim being used to hold the fulminate priming as well as providing means for extracting the cartridge shell.[2] In 1856, Smith and Wesson bought the Rollin White

---

[2]This development probably provided Tyler Henry, Spencer, and others with the idea of making large-calibered, self-contained, rim-fire metallic cartridges which could be used in a number of breech-loading rifles, carbines, and single-shot pistols. Only two steps were left to bring the metallic cartridge shell to its present form: the solid head brass casing and the removable center-fire primer. (See illustration, page 47)

patent of 1855 covering a "bored through cylinder" in revolvers; and thus, with their new .22 caliber cartridge, produced the first breech-loading metallic cartridge revolver in America. The patent enabled them to control the market for this type weapon in the United States until 1869. To get around the patent, many "front-loading" metallic cartridges with inside priming were devised to receive the blow of the hammer at various places: pointed base, inside or cupped base, exterior rib — any scheme to avoid the bored through cylinder loading from the breech.

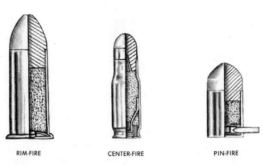

RIM-FIRE   CENTER-FIRE   PIN-FIRE

Various Types of Primed Cartridges

VOLCANIC MAGAZINE PISTOL AND ITS
SELF-CONTAINED CARTRIDGE

Smith and Wesson also had developed the "Volcanic" breech-loading pistol from the older Jennings gun. Like the guns using paper cartridges, the Volcanic used a so-called self-consuming or combustible cartridge, which meant that its discharge left nothing in the barrel, i.e. no shell to be ejected. The cartridge, however, was only an elongated leaden ball with a hollow base in which the powder and percussion primer were placed. These balls were loaded into the muzzle end of a tubular magazine, point foremost, with a torsional gate there being provided for this purpose. By a lever underneath the frame, the balls were transferred one by one from the magazine into the chamber. In the

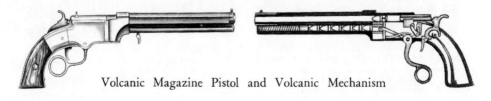

Volcanic Magazine Pistol and Volcanic Mechanism

early pistols the hammer had to be cocked each time before operating the ring lever. Since there was no real seal at the breech and the explosive was limited to a small amount by its bullet cavity, not much effective power was given to the bullet. The weapon never was a commercial success.

THE COMPLETE METALLIC CARTRIDGE: THE
PERFECT GAS SEAL AND THE MAGAZINE
JOIN HANDS

Discounting the exceptional oddities, in single-barreled weapons all non-primed cartridges had to be loaded and fired one by one. In decided contrast, regardless of its deficiencies, the self-primed, lead-ball cartridge of the Volcanic pistol could be loaded and fired in repetition from a tubular magazine. Now came this new self-primed metallic cartridge by Flobert, improved by Smith and Wesson, round in form with no pins or other irregular projections to interfere with handling it in a tubular magazine. Its possibilities were clearly evident.

But more important, the metallic cartridge not only provided a single, complete, sturdy load for the breechloader, but when fired the shell case expanded to absolutely seal the chamber against leakage of powder gas to the rear. And the cartridge, due to its rugged and safe structure, could be handled in magazines of any practical shape or type, fed to the gun chamber, fired, and the empty shell extracted thus making the gun ready for mechanical repetition of the same cycle.

HENRY'S INVENTIONS, 1860

About 1860, Tyler Henry developed a .44 caliber rim-fire cartridge for the Volcanic mechanism which he had adapted to a rifle with a hand lever by which the loading motion simultaneously cocked the hammer. He also redesigned the piston-bolt to carry a two-pronged firing pin for his rim-fire cartridge and means for extracting and ejecting the empty shell in the same motion. His rim-fire cartridge had considerable power and the old Volcanic mechanism, now employed in the new Henry rifle, found quick favor commercially because of its ability to fire rapidly the fifteen shots in its tubular magazine.[3] But

[3]See illustration, page 57.

U. S. Ordnance Bureau was unimpressed. With King's improvement in 1866 for loading the magazine from a gate in the receiver at the rear, the Henry became the Winchester Repeating Rifle which as a repeater made more history and was produced in more models than any other American rifle up to 1900.

THE MINIÉ BALL, 1851

In the early 1850's this period of change also gave attention to the projectile. Conical rifle balls instead of the round balls were coming into use. Because of their superior accuracy (as Walker told Colt) for expanding the balls into the rifling with more certainty and precision, the conical balls compelled attention. One invention in particular, that of Captain C. E. Minié of the French army in 1851, appeared cheap and effective. It used a tapered plug in the hollow base of the ball so that when the charge was fired the expanding gas drove the plug farther into the bullet thus forcing into the rifling the thin edge of the bullet base. James H. Burton, of the Harpers Ferry Armory, found that the gas pressure alone was sufficient to expand the bullet base and, therefore, that the tapered plug was unnecessary. Nevertheless, the idea of the "means" for this purpose was Captain Minié's and so his name stuck to the invention.

MAYNARD TAPE PRIMER AND METALLIC CARTRIDGE, 1845-1857

Some years previously, in 1845, Edward Maynard, a dentist of Washington, D. C., had invented a percussion tape primer similar to those made for the ordinary toy cap pistol of the present day. In a similar way the tape was pushed forward one percussion space each time the hammer was cocked, thus placing the sealed-in bit of percussion powder above the hole in the detonating cone or nipple. Unlike the ordinary copper cap, the gun could be primed with the same speed in the dark as in daylight; and no bits of the copper cap would fly back into one's face at the explosion. But rain or much moist weather constantly threatened the tape, so copper caps also were needed. Doctor Maynard later invented a metallic cartridge with a copper case having a wide rim for easy extraction but not self-primed. Instead, there was a small hole in the base to take the priming flash from his tape primer or from the usual copper percussion cap. He was the first American inventor to formally claim that his cartridge effectively sealed the breech. But not being self-primed, when the rim-fired cartridge appeared on the market, it soon lost importance.

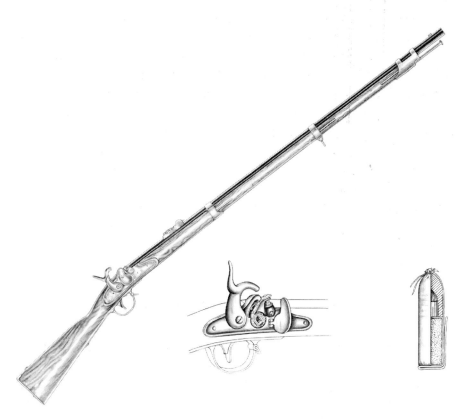

U. S. Model 1855, Rifle Musket; Maynard's Tape Primer; and Minié Ball

MODEL 1855 RIFLE-MUSKET AND OTHER TAPE PRIMED PIECES[4]

Using the Minié ball described above and the tape primer invented by Maynard, the Springfield and Harpers Ferry Armories in 1855 produced a new rifle-musket of caliber .58. The Springfield Armory

[4]See footnote 12, page 43.

also produced a pistol with the same tape primer, this pistol having a detachable stock. About ten years before this, a Pennsylvania contractor had applied the tape primer to government muskets for trial. Also Massachusetts Arms Company had applied it to both types, large and small, of the English Adams revolver they were making under license. Remington received a government contract for a so-called Model 1857 to apply the tape primer to 20,000 flintlock muskets being altered to percussion. During Colonel George Wright's campaign in 1858 against the Spokane, Coeur d'Alene, and Palouse Indians, his command used the Model 1855 .58 caliber rifle-musket with great success. As a result, during the early part of the Civil War, the Union army was armed largely with the Model 1855 rifle-musket using the Minié ball. Very often, however, the regulation copper cap was used in preference to the tape primer because of deterioration due to moisture, and therefore, from 1860, the tape-primer rifle was replaced gradually by new guns without it. But just as important, perhaps more so, was the war need of simplifying and thus speeding up manufacture by adopting plain locks and musket caps to accord with the older patterns largely in use.

RIVALS OF COLT'S REVOLVERS

Due to the expiration of the Colt revolver patent, extended to 1857, there were now in 1860 many other percussion revolvers available or soon to be available, such as Remington (a very rugged dependable piece), Whitney, Savage, Starr, Warner, Springfield, Allen & Wheelock, Rogers & Spencer, Manhattan, Metropolitan, Bacon, Cooper, Prescott, Freeman, and Joslyn. Smith & Wesson made no martial size revolvers until 1870. English percussion revolvers imported before the Civil War, and by both sides during it, were: Adams, Kerr, Deane — all .44 caliber; and Tranter .36 caliber. From France came the principal metallic cartridge revolver, the Lefaucheux 11 m/m, which was also used later in the war by both North and South. France also supplied the American invented LeMat ten-shot percussion revolver — nine shots of 9 m/m (.38 caliber) in the cylinder which rotated on a hollow journal also serving as an under barrel of 20 gauge or .615 caliber for a load of buckshot as a final blast if all else failed. The shift from revolver fire to the under barrel was by means of an adjustable striking nose on the hammer, an idea which again is being used today on a new dual-purpose revolver.

THE COLT ARMY .44, 1860

In 1860, Colt produced a new model Army revolver which, because of its heavier caliber, was to prove perhaps the most popular of all percussion revolvers, not excluding even the Model 1851 Navy. This new Army revolver probably had more use on both sides in the Civil War by cavalry and guerrillas than any other. Southerners were always keen to capture them from the Union cavalry as well as their Spencer carbines of which more comment in a moment.

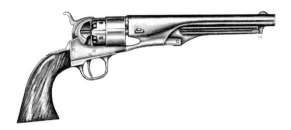

Colt Army, Model 1860, Revolver

In 1861, Colt duplicated the new Army model with a similar Navy model in .36 caliber. Also the Colt factory in recent years had been producing Root side-hammer rifles and revolvers with a rib over the cylinder which thereby made a solid frame especially desirable for these heavy-calibered revolving rifles used in the war.

NEW BREECHLOADERS FOR THE NEW METALLIC CARTRIDGE, 1860-1865

Throughout the years just preceding and during the Civil War, the growing popularity of the breechloader caused many new ones to be produced, the great majority in carbine form for the use of mounted troops and for the use of the new metallic cartridge. This type of cartridge was not only waterproof, but it was fast to handle and could withstand rough treatment. The earlier breechloaders, if the breech-loading method was suitable, were altered to use the metallic cartridge. Sharps was one of these. There were over thirty effective carbines including the Spencer.[5] Of all this number, though others used the *complete* metallic cartridge, the Spencer was the outstanding weapon because of its fast underlever action and its seven-shot tubular magazine in the butt quickly refilled with a loaded tube from the Blakeslee carrier. The carrier contained seven to ten tubes of sheet metal, each tube holding seven cartridges. After the magazine had been withdrawn from the butt of the carbine, the seven cartridges in the tube could be poured by gravity into the magazine cavity in the butt. Then the spring-operated tubular magazine was inserted and locked into the butt plate, thus activating the new reload in one movement. However the hammer had to be cocked for each shot; and the inventor had to go to President Lincoln in the early days of the war to get any action. Together, the President and the inventor fired it successfully at a shingle, and with equal success, teamed up for its adoption.

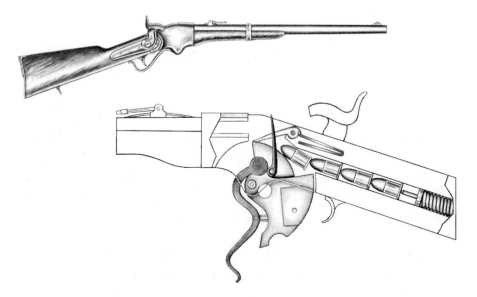

Spencer Carbine, 1860; and Spencer Loading Mechanism

[5]Some of the more important were: Burnside, Maynard, Merrill, Greene, Ball, Smith, Joslyn, Palmer, Starr, Union or Cosmopolitan, Gallager, Triplett & Scott, Sharps & Hankins, and Remington.

THE SPENCER AND THE HENRY

The Spencer was the carbine which the "Rebs" accused the "Yanks" of "loading on Sunday to shoot all week." But there are other claimants. By purchase out of their own pockets, two Illinois Veteran Volunteer regiments armed themselves with the Henry rifle before joining Sherman on his "march to the sea." On this march it is stated that the same remark about unlimited magazine capacity was also attributed to the Henry rifle. But the Spencer, because of its far greater use in the war, appears to have a better claim to the distinction. The United States bought only about 1700 Henry rifles. The only military units for which the Henry rifle was issued by the federal government seem to be the First District Cavalry in Washington, D. C., commanded by the head of the Secret Service, Colonel LaFayette C. Baker, eight companies of the 1st Maine Cavalry, and possibly the 12th Kentucky Cavalry. However, several of the states bought a considerable number. Most of the Civil War carbines in service, and of course the Henry rifle, used rim-fire metallic cartridges; and, except for the Henry, they were largely of .50 or .52 caliber.

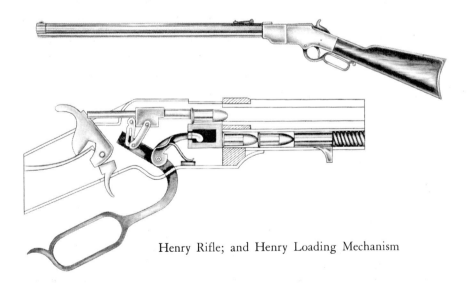

Henry Rifle; and Henry Loading Mechanism

The carbine breech closure methods were of many types: blocks which slid up or down; gates which pivoted to the right or left; barrels which tilted up at the breech or slid forward by means of levers underneath or latches on top; latchable bolts hinged at front or rear; and sliding bolts, of which two levered or rocked the cartridges successively from a tubular magazine underneath the barrel; and one, in 1865, a turn bolt with a separate hammer which was the first bolt action breech purchased for United States armed forces. This was the Palmer.

CIVIL WAR DEMANDS FOR FIREARMS

In the Civil War, losses by damage, excitement, or capture in battle were considerable. For example, after the Battle of Gettysburg, over 35,000 guns were picked up, and, of these, great numbers contained more than one load each — a few with four or more — of unfired cartridges. This, of course, applies only to the muzzle-loading muskets and rifles.[6] Thus in addition to the arming of thousands of new recruits, always there were the battle losses to be replaced. For all these demands, the Springfield Armory, with a yearly capacity in 1864 of 250,000, was the main reliance of the North, backed by the guns supplied by private contractors such as Remington; Whitney; Colt; Parker, Snow & Company; and many others. The Harpers Ferry Armory had been lost to the South early in the war and the machinery there shipped to the Richmond Armory and to Fayetteville, North Carolina, where it soon commenced to serve the Confederacy. Still, for over two years the demand everywhere was greater than the supply.

Smith & Wesson No. 2 Revolver and "Hammond Bull Dog" Pistol

[6]After Gettysburg, 37,574 muskets (all types Union and Confederate, smooth and rifled) were picked up. Of 24,000 found loaded, 6,000 had one load each, 12,000 had two loads, 5,999 had three to ten loads, and one had 23 loads. Had any of the guns with over three loads been fired, they would very likely have blown up. Some had untorn cartridges and some had the cartridges upside down — in some instances with the ball of the first load at the cap nipple, thus preventing discharge of the gun. The result of these disclosures was to advance the adoption of the breechloader which occurred soon after the war ended.

Even converted flintlocks had to be pressed into use; and at times in the South flintlocks in original form were used. The need for belt holster arms had to be satisfied in the early days of the war by single-shot muzzleloaders, while the personal purchase of small-calibered firearms was a common thing for both officers and men. For this, the new Smith & Wesson No. 2 revolver of .32 rim-fire caliber with six-inch barrel, and the .41 rim-fire single-shot "Hammond Bull Dog", were favorites in the North.

Enfield Rifle (made by Barnett, London)

Consequently the hundreds of thousands of volunteers and recruits flocking to military camps on both sides for the Civil War caused a scramble all over Europe for military weapons. Of course upon both the North and the South, the two competing purchasers, there was unloaded a considerable amount of inferior or second-rate ordnance just as in manpower, the North had to contend with the "Bounty Jumpers." The best foreign military rifle to be had was the British Enfield .577 caliber, close enough to the standard U. S. caliber .58 to permit ammunition being interchangeable. During the war, North and South together imported about half a million of these death dealers which without fear or favor spoke their piece for the side they served.

MILITARY LESSONS

There were numerous military lessons to be drawn from the Civil War, but many of them got little attention until long after. It was the first great war to be fought with the tools of the Industrial Revolution. It was a testing ground for new weapons. The long range rifles and artillery, with their increased firepower, were forcing changes in time honored tactics which still would take much blood-letting before the world could see the light. There were many competent observers from Europe accompanying the armies of both North and South, but few of these properly assessed the long range import of what they saw.

One of the great lessons had been in progress for more than one hundred years. It covered two main trends. With constant improvement in accuracy, range (distance), and rate of fire, the first trend was the growing effectiveness of the rifle itself — a purely mechanical and ballistical thing. The second trend was the human element in noting this effectiveness, in determining its capability in battle and in designing tactical methods of putting this capability to practical use. Commencing with the Braddock affair in 1755, there are a regular succession of impressive events: the Plains of Abraham; Virginia riflemen at Norfolk and other places; Morgan's riflemen at Saratoga, Kings Mountain, Cowpens; the Plain of Chalmette at New Orleans; Davis' Mississippians at Buena Vista; and, finally here in the Civil War, Fredericksburg, Antietam, Gettysburg, the "Bloody Angle" at Spottsylvania, Cold Harbor, Petersburg.

All of these conflicts were demonstrating, time and again, that men massed in close order cannot successfully attack the rifle behind a prepared defense line unless that line is flanked or otherwise neutralized. In contrast to the old-time smoothbore musketry, infantry could not get close enough to the rifle to make the bayonet effective in frontal attack. And finally, the rifle forced the artillery back into positions, well behind the infantry front instead of on line with it or perhaps at times in front of it as had been the well-grounded custom.

Illustrative of the rapidly growing dominence of the rifle, the Confederate defense of the stone wall at Fredericksburg caused a Union loss of 6300 in dead, wounded, and missing. Another stone wall at Gettysburg gave Pickett's 15,000 almost an equal loss, his charge being broken at the finish by less than half his number of the Union Second Corps behind the wall. Burnside commanded the Union army attack at Fredericksburg, getting one man within thirty feet of the wall. Lee commanded the Confederate army attack at Gettysburg, getting 150 men over that wall, all being killed or captured. It was a ghastly bountiful harvest for the Springfield and Enfield rifles. In this three-day battle, the high tide of the Confederacy, the combined total loss for both sides was about 50,000 men.[7]

In this same State of Pennsylvania from its humble beginning in the Lancaster area to the grisly fields of Gettysburg only fifty miles away, the American rifle had come a long way, though by this time there were others. But American rifle history was still in the making. With the advent of smokeless powder and the clip magazine, both originating in Europe, another page would unfold.

[7]Pickett's charge was an approach march for most of the distance covered in the mile advance. His front was a mile long and consisted of ten brigades, six in the front line and four behind — more than 15,000 men from Longstreet's Corps including the three brigades of Pickett's own division. Pickett commanded the entire force which amounted to almost one-fourth of Lee's entire army. In the final phase of their course, the men were actually charging; and Pickett's own division of about 4500 men (less losses) was in the forefront, being met at the stone wall by the Second Corps of the Union army which stopped the charge. Less than a third of these brave men were able to rejoin Lee's army, the loss in retreat being greater perhaps than in the advance.

CHAPTER VI

FROM 1865 TO THE END OF THE
SPANISH-AMERICAN WAR

After the Civil War, of course all firearms makers, both military and civilian, rapidly adopted the metallic cartridge. This cartridge, too, was improved for ignition by changing the larger calibers from rim to center fire — at first non-reloadable but soon made so that the small exposed cap in the center of the cartridge base could be removed after firing and replaced by a new one. To strengthen these larger calibers, within ten years, the cartridge shells were made of brass instead of copper with a solid head for center-fire caps. By finding methods of drawing the shell cases to longer lengths, thus permitting larger powder charges, the range of the weapons was greatly increased.

Government arsenals also had the problem of remodeling the thousands of muskets and rifles into practical cartridge weapons. Many methods of altering these obsolete muzzleloaders to use breech-loading metallic cartridges were devised. After various trials, the one selected was that of E. S. Allin, Master Armorer of the Springfield Armory, which in 1866 was made with a so-called lift-up or "trap-door" breech-block accommodating a new .50 caliber center-fire cartridge using 70 grains of black powder. To use the old .58 caliber rifle barrels for this, the breech end was cut off, the rifling reamed out, and a new .50 caliber rifled tube brazed into the old barrel. Then a new breech end, with its latchable, front-hinged breechblock, was fastened to the old barrel. This same breech system in various models of carbine and rifle, one with a ramrod bayonet, was used until the Spanish-American War; and even during that war by some of the state troops called into federal service.

WYOMING, 1867 — BREECHCLOUT MEETS
BREECHLOADER

But the Model 1866 Springfield soon had a test in the field which was severely practical. This was the Wagon Box Fight which took place in the summer of 1867 near old Fort Phil Kearny.[1] Because it never had been used in combat, this new breech-loading Springfield recently supplied to the garrison was unknown to the Indians. The infantry had long been armed with the muzzleloader which after a shot or two might be ridden down in one fast charge of Indian cavalry — named by more than one regular army cavalryman, "the finest in the world." When the breechblock of the new breechloader was raised, it flipped out the cartridge case, loaded or empty. Compared to its muzzle-loading parent, this rifle was several times faster, more accurate, and had a range of more than a half mile.

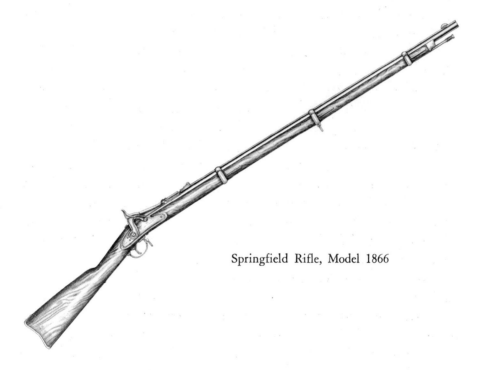

Springfield Rifle, Model 1866

[1]In a way, the Wagon Box Fight exacted some penalty for the Fetterman disaster of the preceding December which cost the lives of Colonel Fetterman and his entire command — two officers, Brown and Grummond; 79 enlisted men; and two civilians, frontiersmen Wheatly and Fisher, each armed with a Henry rifle. The effectiveness of their Henrys was evident from the ground which was sprinkled with empty shells and, farther out, great gouts of blood from the dead and wounded Indians who had been carried off by their fellows.

There were thirty infantrymen under the command of Captain James Powell, an ante bellum sergeant of Dragoons. They occupied a corral of wagon boxes laid flat on the ground, the running gear being used by two wood-fuel cutting parties for which these infantrymen were acting as a central guard. The corral also served as a storage of extra supplies for the working parties and included surplus rifles and ammunition.

The Sioux and Cheyenne began by attacking the mule herders and stampeding the mules of the woodcutters. Captain Powell led a sortie which enabled the herders to join the armed working parties which then retreated to the Fort. In the skirmish two woodcutters joined Powell thus increasing his corral defenders to thirty-two men.

The attack on the corral began about nine in the morning and lasted with some intermissions until early afternoon. The Indians first charged with full confidence that they could ride right over the corral in spite of the expected volley or two from the few defenders. Instead, they charged within one hundred yards before the corral responded with a never ending lethal blast of smoking flashes. In this way they came within short range of these powerful rifles before they realized that they were facing something entirely new. At such close range, the .50 caliber balls easily made casualties of two or more Indians if they happened to be close behind one another. However, with admirable courage, in different ways during the day, the Indians made six charges. Many defending rifle barrels became so hot that they were useless and thus dropped for a fresh gun.

With six casualties the working parties reached Fort Phil Kearny and reported the fight at the corral. A relief party was sent with a howitzer. The Indians, satiated by their several attacks on the corral, promptly retired. Captain Powell estimated the Indian loss at 67 killed and 120 wounded. Most of his men who made a statement placed the loss at between three and four hundred.[2] Powell's own loss was Lieutenant Jenness and one private killed and two privates severely wounded. Long after the fight, the Indians called it the "Bad Medicine Fight of the White Man." One said they lost over 1000 braves — "they never fought again"; (meaning the total of killed, wounded, and otherwise incapacitated).[3]

---

[2]George A. Forsyth, *The Story of the Soldier* (New York, 1900), pp. 157-8.
[3]Cyrus Townsend Brady, *Indian Fights and Fighters* (New York, 1905), pp. 54-6.

COLORADO, 1868 — THE SPENCER CARBINE
AND THE COLT WIN AGAIN

The next year, September, 1868, there was a fight on the Arikaree Fork of the Republican River in northeastern Colorado, which adds to the annals of bravery and courage for both red man and white. It was fought with the unaltered weapons of the Civil War on a little island in the river afterward named Beecher's Island for one of the officers killed in the struggle. The island defenders were a body of fifty scouts, mostly ex-soldiers, enlisted as quartermaster's employees for technical reasons but serving as scouts under Colonel George A. Forsyth. Afterward they were called, by certain writers, the "Rough Riders of '68." They were equipped of course as cavalry, their arms being a Spencer repeating carbine and a Colt .44 percussion revolver to each man. For the carbine, they carried 144 rounds and, for the revolver, thirty rounds of ammunition per man with 4000 extra rounds on pack mules.

After many days trailing Indian movements, the command was camped on the north bank of the Arikaree Fork. In the half light of early dawn, discovering that they were surrounded except for the river side, they opened fire. By this alarm the Indians were stopped just short of stampeding all their animals. Forsyth at once moved the command to the island opposite in the midst of the shallow stream. Then he had the men dig small individual defense pits with knives and mess kits. The Indians kept up a brisk fire with repeating rifles; and Forsyth's horses and mules commenced to drop, or wounded they had to be shot thus providing additional cover. The scouts returned the fire of the Indians on the opposite bank, deliberately and carefully to conserve the ammunition. After some minutes, the Indians, having lost a number of men because they were the more exposed, retired out of rifle range. Forsyth estimated the Indian force at several hundred Cheyenne and Sioux, while his chief scout Grover said there were a thousand all under command of a very large Indian chief called Roman Nose.[4]

The manner in which the Indians drew off around a bend in the stream caused Forsyth to guess that they were organizing a charge to

---

[4]The term chief applied here to Roman Nose is only a title of convenience because there are differences of interpretation as to his actual tribal status.

ride right over his scanty intrenchments. So the guns, including those of the killed and the severely wounded, were loaded to capacity; and the revolvers were all examined for loads and proper capping, being left loose in the holsters. The men were ordered to lie low until the word was given, when they should face the charge.

The Indian horsemen soon swept around the bend with a front of about sixty men and a depth of six or eight ranks. The warriors, with the exception of cartridge belt and box and mocassins, were perfectly naked and hideously painted. They rode with only a single horse-hair lariat running twice around the horse's belly and passing loosely over each knee. Their hair was braided and scalp locks festooned with feathers or covered with a war bonnet. Guiding their mounts with the bridle in the left hand, they held their rifles squarely across the fronts of their bodies, some resting on the necks of the horses. The rising ground out of range on the north bank was covered with Indian women and children spectators.

Riding well in front, Roman Nose led the charge with reckless gallantry. Forsyth called him "the very beau ideal of an Indian chief."[5] As soon as the charge started, the Indians, hidden on both banks opposite the island, opened a rapid fire to cover the movement and keep the scouts from fighting it off. But the thrice wounded Forsyth held back the word until the charge was close enough to mask the Indian support fire from the opposite river banks.

At the right moment Forsyth shouted. His men rose with their Spencers ready and sent "seven successive crashing volleys into the savage horde."[6] At the first and second volleys, with a wild yell, the Indians came gallantly on. The third volley cut short their shouts. There were gaps in their ranks, and men and horses were going down in the shallows. But Roman Nose still led, waving his heavy Springfield rifle over his head. The fourth volley seemed to slow him; the charge hesitated but still came on. The fifth volley appeared to pile carcasses in heaps. "At the sixth, Roman Nose and his horse went down in death together."[7] As some of the warriors reached the foot of the little island, the seventh and last volley was fired. Then springing to their feet, the scouts with cheers poured a rapid revolver fire fairly into the faces of

---

[5]Forsyth, *op. cit.*, p. 223.
[6]*Ibid.*, p. 224.
[7]*Ibid.*, p. 225.

these remaining dauntless riders. The Indian column divided on each side of the island and sought the safety of the opposite shores. Later in the day, the Indians tried two more charges but were easily beaten off.

That night, Forsyth sent off messengers to get help. The command, besieged for nine days, existed on dead horse and mule meat (at the end fairly putrid) until relief came. Forsyth lost two officers killed, and eight men badly and ten slightly wounded — a casualty list of forty per cent.[8] Every animal he had was killed except seven stampeded by the Indians. His report stated that the Indians "were splendidly armed with Spencer and Henry rifles."[9]

METALLIC CARTRIDGE REVOLVERS

For hand weapons, the changeover to the cartridge was a little slower because of the Smith & Wesson ownership of the Rollin White patent for bored-through cylinders. In 1871, Smith & Wesson brought out their first martial, a .44 caliber "top-break", simultaneous ejecting revolver made for the Russian government.

Smith & Wesson Russian Model Revolver, 1871

[8]Stanley Vestal (Professor W. S. Campbell), who died about three years ago, was a close student and researcher among the Plains Indians. He wrote many books and articles from the Indian viewpoint. For both the Wagon Box and Beecher Islands fights, he gave the Indian dead at perhaps six or eight for each fight. In view of the official reports and figures, I could not accept Vestal's figures made so long after the events took place and wrote him so. At the same time, I asked if by some means such as presents, etc., he had not indicated to the Indian interviewed an idea of the nature of the information expected or desired. He denied absolutely any such possibility. But see *Montana, the Magazine of Western History,* VIII (April, 1958), wherein Vestal's close friend, Maurice Frink, wrote an article titled "A Little Gift for Last Bull." Furthermore, the Indian has reason for pride in racial prowess. Thus it would be natural for descendants either to magnify Indian prowess or to minimize Indian losses.

[9]Forsyth, *op. cit.,* p. 229. Forsyth, however, states specifically that Roman Nose carried a Springfield.

When the Smith & Wesson patent expired in 1869, plans already underway by rival manufacturers promptly brought on the market several other good breech-loading revolvers like the Colt and the Remington altered from percussion front loaders to use the .38 and .44 caliber rim-fire and center-fire cartridges.

The complete Colt alteration was accomplished by removing the percussion rammer lever and latch; plugging the ram hole in the barrel lug; removing the cap cones and cutting back the chambers above the cylinder ratchet; installing a new recoil plate or standing breech (with loading gate) to fill the cap cone space, with allowance for the heads of the metallic cartridges; and altering the hammer with a longer nose to reach these cartridges for either rim or center fire as the case might be. Some instead carried a rebounding firing pin in the recoil plate. A cartridge ejection rod was added to the right side of the barrel.

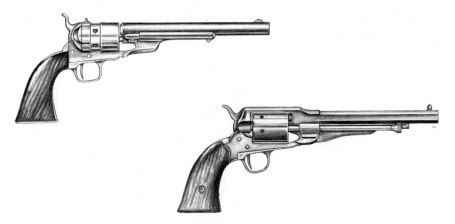

Percussion Revolvers Altered to Use Center-fire Cartridges:
Colt and Remington

The Remington alteration of its army revolver affected only the cylinder and the hammer. The old percussion cylinder was replaced by a new one made expressly for the metallic cartridge; and the nose of the hammer was altered to fire (usually) center-fire cartridges. A cartridge ejector rod was added to the right side of the frame and alongside the barrel.

The new Remington of 1875 looked much like the altered Remington because it carried a piece under the barrel similar to the old rammer lever. To this piece was affixed the cartridge ejector rod.

But the Colt issue of 1873, its first basic metallic cartridge revolver, was the most durable, popular, and fascinating in public memory, due to its association with the "Old Army", the frontier cowboy, badman, sheriff, and Indian. This was the single-action center-fire Colt .45 widely known as the "Peacemaker" which brings to the forefront two Indian struggles wherein it received its "Old Army" baptism: the Custer Battle and the Nez Perce War.

Colt Army, Model 1873, "Peacemaker"

MONTANA, 1876 — STORED GATLINGS AND SOFT CARBINE FODDER RUIN CUSTER'S 7th

The National Centennial celebration in 1876 had one memorable blot when, on June 25, General George A. Custer, the dashing cavalry leader with long, yellow hair, famous youngster of the Civil War, with five troops of the 7th Cavalry, was wiped out completely by Sioux and Cheyenne Indians on the Little Big Horn River in Montana. In death he took with him his two brothers and a nephew. The combined loss of all troops of the 7th Cavalry in the general engagement was 270 killed and 53 wounded. The Indian loss has been stated to have totaled about 70; and one account, from the Indian view, gives a total of 32.

For a general attack on the large Indian encampment, Custer had divided his force into three parts probably with the same feeling shared by Colonel Fetterman ten years earlier, i.e. with a small command of good cavalry, he could ride right through the entire Sioux nation. So behind him he left the Gatling machine guns which might have won for him all he had hoped to gain. On the other hand, he was striving for speed and mobility.

After marching all night, at 8 a.m. he was on one of the creeks flowing into the Little Big Horn. Taking personal command of Troops C, E, F, I, and L, he marched down the right bank of the stream leading to the river. About 11 a.m., Major Marcus A. Reno, with Troops A, G, and M, was ordered to attack the Indian village now reported on the left bank of the river about two miles away. Custer continued downstream to take it in flank. At first the Indians feigned a retirement before Reno's advance until near the village when they came boiling back at him like a swarm of angry hornets.

At this time Reno could neither see nor hear anything of Captain Benteen, who was supposed to be scouting the left flank with Troops H, D, and K, or of Custer, who by this time should be crossing the river in the supporting flank attack on the village. Reno saw, however, that the village instead of containing several hundred up to one thousand Indians as expected was only part of a much larger encampment. His troops had been dismounted to form a firm battle line. But, with the Indian masses threatening his flanks and rear, he mounted his command; haphazardly charged through the Indian swarms, mounted and afoot; recrossed the river; and secured a defense position on the bluffs above. In this affair he lost 3 officers and 29 enlisted men killed and 7 others wounded. At this place on the bluffs, Captain Benteen, with three troops, and Captain McDougall, with Troop B and the pack train, joined Major Reno. No word had come from Custer except a message to Benteen: "Come on. Big Village. Bring packs. P.S. Bring packs."[10]

Some firing had been heard downstream but now all was quiet. Captain Weir went with his troop to get information; but Weir was heavily attacked and had to return. Reno then resumed his defense position among the bluffs with his seven troops of cavalry amounting to about 400 officers and men. And there they remained under attack until about nine o'clock that night, Reno losing in these engagements 18 killed and 46 wounded. The Indians resumed their attack about three o'clock the next morning, ending about 9 a.m. when a determined charge by the Indians was met with an equally determined counter charge led by Captain Benteen, which was so unexpected that the

---

[10]The packs contained the extra ammunition. This message was sent to Benteen because Reno was supposed to be at the village.

Indians were confused and completely routed. On the opposite side of the position, Reno also led a counter charge with Troops D and K.

About noon the Indians commenced to draw away toward their villages. The night of the 26th passed quietly and on the next day General Terry arrived with the main command. Two hours later, because there were no survivors, all that was ever to be known of the fate of Custer and his five troops of cavalry was disclosed by examination of the battlefield with its rows of mutilated bodies.

Although there were no survivors, there have been fourteen different stories of dead soldiers or battlefield remnants such as U. S. horses or equipment found at some distances. A few men may have, as claimed, covered themselves with an Indian blanket and in the confusion of the immediate battle gotten away temporarily. This may account for the remains which were found at different times afterward within a few miles of the action.

Since the early technical discussions of this disaster were given to the public about seventy years ago by army officers Edward S. Godfrey and James B. Fry, there have been scores of articles and books dissecting the episode from every angle: personal, political, military, and historical.[11] And until her death in the 1930's, Mrs. Custer, pathetic and appealing, stemmed the flow of narratives derogatory to the General. Today there is little to add.

Aside from the fact that the Gatlings were left behind, the single-shot Springfield carbines in the hands of the men and the repeating rifles in the hands of some of the Indians are things to ponder. Comparatively, the Springfield was a pugilist with one hand. Another thing is that the Springfield had replaced the seven-shot repeating Spencer carbine. The single-shot Model 1873 Springfield was a good piece — with suitable ammunition. But cartridges with a folded head, when over-expanded in a hot gun, often would not extract. In some instances, the extractors tore through the soft rims of the hot shells. The troopers tried to dig out these shells with pocket knives.

In this situation, all that the Colt six-shot Peacemaker could do was to keep the Indians at a distance while the trooper dug away at his Springfield carbine. Dismounted early in the fight, the troopers were in line of battle with no means of maneuver. Therefore, their Colt

[11]Edward S. Godfrey, "Custer's Last Battle", *Century Magazine*, XLIII (January, 1892), 358-84; James S. Fry, "Comments", *Century Magazine*, XLIII (January, 1892), 385-87.

revolvers were not so effective because the Indians rode rapidly about just outside good revolver range, offering difficult targets but still within easy rifle range. In this way these riders were able to cut down the blue ranks while the troopers' carbines became useless due to stuck shells or lack of ammunition. Thus their finish was readily apparent to all.

These estimates of what happened were all conjectural because they were based on the appearance of the battlefield and the shell cases found there. The Indians of course picked up all the serviceable weapons. There are stories, too, that Custer at the end committed suicide with his revolver, but actual evidence is all against this, one of the most important proofs being that there were no powder burns. Several Indian claims have been made for the individual glory of killing Custer.

So we are left with the unforgettable mental picture of devoted regulars, obeying orders to the very last, desperately waiting the end with perhaps one shell reserved in the faithful Colt for a self-inflicted death before the scalping knife reached in. These men died in ranks which marked with admirable regularity for such a struggle their last position of duty and devotion on the dismal slopes above the Little Big Horn.

IDAHO-MONTANA, 1877 — NEZ PERCE, MASTERS OF MOBILITY AND RIFLE

The final Indian struggle for freedom was by a tribe which had been friendly toward the white man since the days of Lewis and Clark, some seventy years past. As an Indian nation, the Nez Perce had stood with the whites while other northern Indians in Oregon and Washington were fidgety, frenetic, and fighting because of the steady inflow of white settlers who came with axes and shovels in their hands to occupy permanently the land. The Nez Perce were people of calm judgment led by far-sighted chiefs. But the steady encroachment finally brought about resistance when their boundaries were compressed by the loss of the Wallowa and Imnaha valleys and they were asked to go to the Lapwai reservation.

The father of the incumbent Chief Joseph together with Chief Looking Glass had signed the Treaty of 1855 because by it they retained these two beautiful valleys. In 1863, another treaty was made which took away those valleys; but old Chief Joseph and other Nez Perce chiefs whose people dwelled there refused to sign. For that refusal, they were called the "Non-Treaty Indians" but by suffrance were allowed to remain there in spite of white settler pressure, with the expectation that the difficulty would be worked out. However, these Nez Perce were so disturbed that in 1873 President Grant, by executive order, gave Chief Joseph and the Nez Perce affected the exclusive use of the Wallowa Valley. In 1875 this order was revoked. In 1876, General O. O. Howard, the Department Military Commander, asked for a commission to decide the controversy. The commission held that since a majority had signed the Treaty of 1863 Chief Joseph and his people should be required to abide by it.

But these Nez Perce indicated that they had no interest in majority rule. Such rule was not their law and they refused to abide by it. In White Bird Canyon a few of their young braves went on a foray, killing some white men. Troops of U. S. Cavalry came to investigate, and fighting spread through the area.

The resulting hegira of this people without any premeditated plan began in June, 1877, on the western slopes of the Bitterroot Range. After crossing these mountains and two other ranges in Wyoming and Montana with eleven brisk fights and over 1200 miles of travel, three months later at the north end of the Bear Paw Range about forty miles from the Canadian line, Chief Joseph spoke the moving words of the surrender.

After the first few fights, amid efforts by both Indians and whites to stop the struggle, the personal leadership was supplied by Chief Joseph. At the start, in addition to nearly 300 warriors, his band included over 200 women and children with a herd of at least 1500 horses and ponies. The women drove the horse herd, did all the camp work, cooked the food, and put up the shelters at night. As the Indians crossed the country ahead of the pursuing soldiers, they swept up all the horses of every ownership so that the soldiers were always short of fresh mounts while the Indians could make faster time whenever necessary. Years later in writing of this campaign, General George A. Forsyth wrote that Chief Joseph showed himself one of the ablest and most astute Indian warriors of the nineteenth century, exhibiting military intuition as to evading pursuers, taking up unassailable positions when attacked, always fighting his forces with sound judgment, and keeping up his flight with a tenacity of purpose little short of marvelous in an untrained savage.[12]

At the surrender the Nez Perce still had about 700 animals most of which were captured by the soldiers. But barely half of Chief Joseph's people were left. About 100 of the warriors had scattered, crept away under cover, and finally crossed the Canadian boundary. In spite of assurances at the surrender that they would be sent back to Idaho, the

[12]Forsyth, op. cit., p. 346. Within the past decade, writings based on Indian points of view have questioned the standing and ability of Chief Joseph as the leader of the Nez Perce breakout in 1877. The sources of these stories were Indians long past their prime or from non-participants who gave hearsay testimony — colored perhaps by pride, jealousy, or other human traits.
Essentially these accounts claim:
1. The Nez Perce had no overall leadership or control.
2. Chief Joseph was no martial man or leader.
3. The real leaders and tacticians, apparently men implied to have had fighting experience, were other Nez Perce chiefs.
4. The success of their long flight was due to the individual prowess of the Indian on the firing line.
5. U. S. Army leaders lavished technical praise on widely known Chief Joseph in order to cloak their own deficiencies.
My own reaction to the above five points is summarized thus:
1. From hundreds of years' experience, the vigorous tribes of Western Indians had developed into natural fighters and tacticians. Like a nest of hornets they needed no indications of an enemy, how to get at him, or how to defend themselves. The Indian was adept in the oldest war tactic, surprise; and he was equally good at guarding against it. Many wars were started by young braves always hard to control, always trying to emulate some prominent warrior, always working to note a gleam of admiration in the bright eyes of the young women of the tribe. The big task for a chief was control.
2. If Chief Joseph was no martial man or leader, where did the other Nez Perce chiefs get their qualifications?
3. The other chiefs did their work well as evidenced by the fighting. As for previous battle experience, where did they get it? There had been no wars in their territory since Wright's campaign of 1858 against the Northern Indians. Even in that war the Nez Perce were not involved.
4. I agree with all claims made as to the individual prowess of the Nez Perce Indian as a fighter. But the success of this remarkable flight was due only in part to these warriors who held off the advance of the soldiers. It has been said that Joseph was rarely on the firing line; that he spent most of his time providing for food, for the movement of the camps, the old men, the wounded, the women and children, the horse herd, for the routes and the timing to be followed. This job was the most difficult of all — the very job which made possible the dramatic flight across Montana. Actually the logistics turn the situation completely around. Two hundred warriors, more or less, fought rear guard or delaying actions while Chief Joseph fed all and moved several hundred women, children, old men, and wounded, with all their equipment, supplies, and an immense horse herd, over a new route to another campsite leading to Canada. Improvised as all this had to be, as a matter of tactical skill, leadership, and timing, I think this is the supreme test. Furthermore, unlike Chief White Bird who deserted his responsibility and stole off to Canada, Chief Joseph did not abandon his people. With his people he drank the bitter tea of defeat; accompanied them into the years of captivity in Oklahoma; and continuously pleading their cause, finally saw them back again on a reservation in their homeland region. This is real leadership.
5. As for U. S. Army officers cloaking their own deficiencies, this accusation might be considered if only one officer was involved. But as a general statement involving three or four well-known officers with honorable records of service including the Civil War, it is absurd. As men of experience, these officers had respect for a chief who was able to feed his people, fight off pursuers, and keep his camps out of harm's way most of the time across Montana.

captives were sent to Oklahoma where they suffered severely by sickness. Finally after seven years, they were returned to the Northwest.

This remarkable flight in the face of three different bodies of U. S. Cavalry which separately or jointly tried to stop them perhaps was due in part to the firearms used by the opposing forces. It is true that at the start on White Bird Creek, the sixty-odd Indians who came at the call of their leaders were partly armed with bows and arrows or muzzle-loading muskets and pistols. But more than half of these warriors had repeating rifles. The troopers, of course, were all armed with the single-shot Springfield carbine and the Colt .45 single-action revolver. General Howard's command also had a howitzer and two Gatling guns. Later, the Indians captured the howitzer, also a quantity of small arms ammunition which they were well able to use in the army carbines they likewise picked up or already had. They also had revolvers some of which had been captured.

One writer stated that the firearms of the soldiers and civilians pursuing the Indians were a sorry lot; whereas the Indians were well armed with rifles made by Sharps, Remington, Ballard, and Winchester, as well as the government Springfield. Much of their plentiful supply of ammunition came from the Crow Indians who dealt with the lawless traders around the buffalo country in Montana.

In actual fighting, the Nez Perce were quick to take advantage of the ground, to secure positions accessible only by frontal attack, to depend mainly on the rifle until the troopers were within close range when the revolver was used effectively by resting the retaining hand or hands on the cover in front. At fifty yards or more the revolver would shoot accurately. With a hand rest it was defensively a serious contender.

The Nez Perce were surprised in camp twice. These attacks were about the only chances the soldiers had to use their revolvers and the Indians in one way or another sustained serious losses.

MORE NEW REVOLVERS

Soon after 1875 the double-action revolver appeared whereby the cocking and firing of the piece were accomplished by a single long pull of the trigger which then was retracted by a spring. This action was a revival and an improvement of that of the early percussion pepperbox, adapted and made durable in the Civil War or later by revolvers such as the Pettengill, the Starr, the Savage, the Remington

Navy, and the Cooper. For breech-loading cartridge revolvers, it was first used in newly designed Smith & Wesson and Colt revolvers, the former in .38 and .44 Frontier models, the latter in the Bisley and lightning models of similar calibers. Before the Spanish-American War both of these leading companies were making still newer models with "swing out" cylinders hung on a crane and providing simultaneous ejection of the cartridges almost as quickly as the "top-break" Smith & Wesson revolver of twenty years before. In addition there were smaller factories such as Forehand & Wadsworth, Iver Johnson, and Harrington & Richardson which made pocket pieces of the same top-break type.

All during this postwar period, from 1870 to 1895 and even later, there was a perfect galaxy of small pocket firearms of every description flooding the market. These were being made in both Europe and America, those from Europe at first being dozens of types of pin-fire revolvers. Many of these little weapons came to be called "Suicide Specials" because of their cheap, fragile, or faulty mechanisms.

EUROPE, 1888: SMOKELESS POWDER

About 1885 the Frenchman Vieille produced in his laboratory the first smokeless powder. This was further improved in 1888 when Nobel, the inventor of dynamite, added guncotton to the mixture. These discoveries immediately attracted world-wide attention. European countries were quick to adapt the commercial product of 1888 to their new military magazine rifles. In the early 1890's a United States Ordnance Board recommended the adoption of the Norwegian Krag-Jorgensen five-shot magazine rifle which used the new smokeless powder. But this recommendation had to wait until United States producers could supply in quantity the new smokeless powder required. The use of this new firearm, therefore, had hardly permeated throughout the regular armed services when the Spanish-American War suddenly erupted. So to some extent the United States was compelled to use the black powder .45-70 Springfield during that war as against a modern, German-designed Mauser magazine rifle using smokeless powder which gave no indication of the location of enemy troops. Thus in the span of a few years, smokeless powder made obsolete all the military weapons, including heavy ordnance, which Americans had been using for 125 years.

It made, also, one other decisive change in military tactics. During the Civil War, several types of quick-firing, mounted, portable, machine guns had been tried. The best of these was the hand-cranked Gatling composed of a rotating nest of barrels to which metallic cartridges were automatically fed from a hopper; but it was not yet completely perfected. Nevertheless it demonstrated in startling fashion the combined importance of these early inventions: Forsyth's percussion powder, Shaw's copper percussion cap, and Flobert's rim-fire cartridge. And now, aside from keeping the gun concealed, smokeless powder in firing was to limit the powder residue from fouling the mechanism and the barrel, so that within the course of a lifetime perfected modern machine guns would be squirting 500 to 1200 rounds per minute.

Smokeless powder worked amazing changes in the hand gun, too. In Europe, Paul Mauser invented his famous machine pistol. And the American John M. Browning, not far behind in his inventive experimental work, produced an automatic pistol which, within a decade of improvement, was accepted by the United States in 1911 as its official service hand weapon. This pistol, in one guise or another, has been copied by many foreign countries.

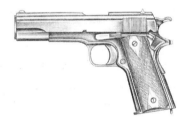

Colt U. S. Army Automatic Pistol, Model 1911

Browning also was a leading inventor of machine guns for the military services of the United States. Some of his earlier weapons have been replaced, only recently, by more effective or lighter mechanisms.

CUBA, 1898: WITH INDIAN WAR WHOOPS, REBEL YELLS, AND BLACKPOWDER, WE BREAK INTO WORLD ORBIT

The Spanish-American War, April-August, 1898, was the outgrowth of a half century of revolts in Cuba. The United States sustained not only great strains and expense in the maintenance of its neutrality, but also enormous losses in trade and commerce. At the same time the United States had to be mindful of the Monroe Doctrine. Nevertheless we had made no preparation for war. Not only did we lack modern small arms, but also we had no field artillery using smokeless powder. We did not fight Spain because we feared her next-door occupation of Cuba. We fought her because of public sympathy for the starving Cubans, their long struggle for freedom without any relief of their burdens by Spain, and because of their appeals to the United States, the world symbol of freedom.

In spite of all these problems, both the United States and Spain made serious efforts to come to some acceptable agreement regarding Cuba. If the United States ·battleship *Maine,* then on a mission of friendship in Havana harbor, had not been blown up, it is possible that war could have been averted.

So in spite of President McKinley's cool handling of this catastrophe, the sinking of the *Maine* precipitated the war which was declared by both parties the third week in April. On May 1, Admiral George Dewey sunk the Spanish fleet in Manila Bay on the other side of the world, with the battle cry "Remember the *Maine.*" Within two months, in Cuba United States troops won the battle of El Caney; "Teddy" Roosevelt and his "Rough Riders" from the West inched their way up San Juan Hill; and Richmond P. Hobson of the Navy with seven men, braving a storm of Spanish shot and shell, unsuccessfully tried to bottle up Spanish Admiral Cervera's fleet in Santiago harbor by sinking a ship in the entrance. On July 3, Cervera's fleet steamed out of the harbor. It was immediately attacked by the American fleet and totally destroyed. Hostilities ceased in August. The treaty of peace provided for the complete independence of Cuba. Puerto Rico, Guam, and the Philippine archipelago became possessions of the United States, and the latter paid Spain $20,000,000 for certain diplomatic claims in connection with the Philippines.[13]

THE FIREARMS, A HISTORICAL MEDLEY. — The firearms used in the Spanish-American War and the Philippine Insurrection which followed were a curious lot from ancient to modern. In Cuba the disparity was not so great as it was later in ·the Philippines. The Spanish in Cuba used the 7 m/m Mauser which was a five-shot, clip-fed, high power rifle using smokeless powder which obviously did not disclose by smoke signal its location. The Cuban insurgents

---

[13]E. Benjamin Andrews, *History of the United States* (New York, 1914); David S. Muzzey, *The American People* (New York, 1932).

used any weapon they could obtain, from the machete or long bladed knife used for harvesting sugar cane, to captured Mauser and Remington rifles (carbine preferred): commercial weapons of all types, shoulder or side-arms, smuggled in from the United States and other countries; and also hunting guns formerly used in peaceful sports. The Remington was the single-shot Spanish Remington of .43 caliber formerly the top official arm of the Spanish army. This was the same "rolling block" breech first introduced by Remington in 1865-1866.

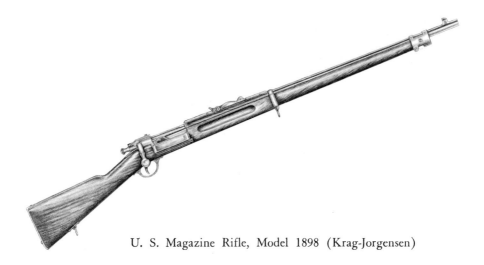

U. S. Magazine Rifle, Model 1898 (Krag-Jorgensen)

The United States regular soldier usually was armed with the five-shot, side-door magazine .30 caliber Krag-Jorgensen rifle, the new service arm using smokeless powder. Although not as good mechanically as the Spanish Mauser, it was a powerful and accurate weapon. For those required to have side-arms, the Colt double-action .38 caliber, six-shot revolver, Model of 1895, was regulation. This had a "swing-out" cylinder carried by a latchable crane with simultaneous ejection of shells. In some engagements, the army also used the Gatling machine gun, hand cranked, with fair success. Men on the warships of the Navy, who were designated to use small arms, carried the Lee "straight pull" 6 m/m rifle which had a non-rotating bolt unlocked by a pull straight to the rear. It was made by Winchester Repeating Arms Company. At the time it was the smallest bore, high velocity rifle using smokeless powder. On some ships also were a few of the old single-shot, "trap door", breech-loading 45-70 Springfield rifles.

Except for cavalry like the "Rough Riders", the volunteer U. S. soldiers, particularly those of the National Guard, were armed with the 45-70 Springfield — the so-called "charcoal burner" of Indian war days. These boys had to blast away at hidden targets kept concealed by smokeless powder regardless of the volume of fire, while every shot out of the Springfield put up a smoke signal visible through binoculars miles away.

Remington Rolling Block Army Rifle

Made for the Spanish Government

So far as concerned United States and Spanish troops in the Philippines, the small arms carried were about the same as in Cuba. Later fighting with the Filipino *Insurrectos* under Aguinaldo marked several differences. From Spanish sources, the *Insurrectos* had gained possession of many of the single-shot .43 caliber, Spanish Remington rifles — the usual "rolling block" type. This rifle used a cartridge known as the *Reformado* which being loaded with smokeless powder had plenty of power and fair velocity. To avoid the shearing of lead from the bullet during its fast passage through the bore, like the high velocity Mauser and Krag bullets it was covered with a jacket of harder metal. However this *Reformado* bullet jacket was of coppery brass which as it gathered moisture produced verdigris or Paris Green all over its exposed surface. When these balls wounded anyone, the verdigris naturally added poison to the wound with evil results. From this fact, the bullet soon was called the "Poison Bullet."

An unusual thing developed in fighting *Insurrecto* guerillas. The Moros and Isorots were exceedingly tough and rugged hill-tribes from the interior. It was soon found that they were so tough that the regulation .38 caliber Colt revolver bullet would not stop them. They might be hit in the body, keep on fighting, and then disappear to fight another day. So the War Department shipped as replacements for the .38 D. A. Colt, the Alaska Model, double action, .45 Colt which has the big trigger guard for use with mittens. This Alaska Model was the only .45 then available and its trigger guard was no handicap. The .45 proved its value as of old. When any man was struck with one of those big slugs, he stayed down.

The Filipinos also used a medley of ancient Spanish guns including many small bronze cannon some of which may be seen on display in various museums. The DeYoung Memorial Museum in San Francisco has one example. Supporting their firearms, the Filipino guerrillas also used knives of all types: the bolo, the Malay kris, and various kinds of Oriental dirks or daggers. Quite often, these knives were used more skillfully and with deadlier effect than were their firearms.

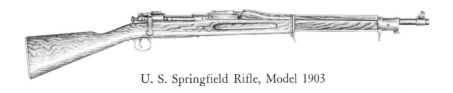

U. S. Springfield Rifle, Model 1903

Following our experiences in the Spanish-American War, the comparative performance of the Krag-Jorgensen rifle as against the German Mauser used by Spain, came under earnest consideration. This resulted in the decision to produce a five-shot magazine military rifle of our own design, suitable in length and weight for all of our martial services. This new rifle became the Springfield Model 1903. In 1906 the cartridge was changed to carry the lighter 150 grain "Spitzer" bullet with a muzzle velocity of 2700 feet per second. In designing the bolt and magazine for the new Springfield, the Mauser action was much preferred. So after some delay, Paul Mauser was paid a sizeable royalty for the use of his patents. Otherwise, this rifle was our own, particularly when thirty years of effort to perfect it are considered.

When discontinued in favor of automatic arms, it was conceded to be the finest and most accurate hand-operated military rifle in the world. Its accuracy fully maintained the reputation af the first "American Rifle", the All-American, Pennsylvania (Kentucky) rifle. The Springfield rifle M1903 is two things: a mechanical device and a precision instrument by reason of its fine rifling especially in the star-gauged barrels. In these barrels the bore is not only exact and perfectly true, but every inch of the rifling down the bore is checked to gauge in thousandths between the lands and to the depths of the grooves. The slightest flaw, spot defect, or lack of polish causes rejection. Therefore the thirty years of effort as illustrated by this one thing, based on over two hundred years of fine rifle making experience in America, is perhaps more important even than the gun mechanism itself.

CHAPTER VII

A NEW CENTURY BEGINNING A
WORLD WIDE FRONTIER

Compared to the larger crises which have occurred since, the Spanish-American War today may seem like an affair of little consequence. Nevertheless it marked the emergence of the United States as a potent force in world leadership. This nation had not had a war with a foreign power for fifty years nor with a European country for eighty-four.

In the preceding century we had acquired the great area between the Mississippi and the Pacific Ocean by negotiation, the Mexican and Indian wars, and by purchase.[1] With the help of millions of immigrants from Europe attracted by the "land of the free and the home of the brave" (eventually symbolized by France's *Independence Centennial* gift of Bartholdi's giant Statue of Liberty in New York harbor),[2] we were populating all that western territory and thus giving hope and opportunity to more millions all over the world.

But the Spanish-American War gave rise to accusations both at home and abroad of imperialism or colonialism based on the feeling that any national increase of power and authority, as shown in the long history of the world, meant the exploitation of weaker peoples. At home the strong argument supporting these accusations, was that any policy of annexing lands already filled with alien peoples could not be reconciled with our Declaration of Independence which insisted upon government "by consent of the governed." The point was made also that the annexation of distant lands in the Pacific Ocean was contrary to the Monroe Doctrine which pledged the United States to confine its political interests to the Western Hemisphere. While some of our people with ideas of greatly increased trade and prosperity in mind overlooked the democratic principles upon which the United States

---

[1]In 1846 we negotiated the Oregon question with England; in 1803 we purchased Louisiana from France; in 1853 we purchased southern portions of Arizona and New Mexico from Mexico; and in 1867 we purchased Alaska from Russia.

[2]Whereas the U. S. Centennial was in 1875, due to the tremendous size of the Statue of Liberty, its transportation from France, and the building of foundations, the erection did not start until 1883 and it took three years to complete. The hand holding the torch was displayed at the Centennial in 1876.

was founded, the great majority stood for independence and freedom for other peoples as well as for those of the United States.

As a consequence, the United States took the position that it acquired the Philippines because Spanish authority there had been destroyed by insurgents supported by American troops; that for commercial reasons, the Phillippines should not fall into the hands of any foreign power; that the Filipinos were then incapable of governing themselves and for a time must be ruled by adequate and humane authority.

The leader of the insurgents was General Emilio Aguinaldo who by Spain had been expelled from the islands, but who had returned with Dewey's victory in Manila Bay. Aguinaldo had besieged Manila from the land side and after its capture by the Americans had set up an independent Philippine government supported perhaps by as many as 30,000 insurgent troops. Soon after, some of these men attacked an American position with initial success but with dire consequences later. This insurrection including its final guerrilla phases carried on without Aguinaldo's support lasted about three years. In the meantime (then) Judge William H. Taft was appointed governor; and internal organizations and improvements, including schools, were started. By 1907 the Filipinos had begun the process of self-government which was to culminate nearly forty years later when they were to rejoice in complete independence.[3]

The progress toward self-government was faster in Cuba where the people were better prepared for it. The United States had to intervene occasionally, but having proved to the Cubans that the island was their independent legacy so long as they could run things effectively and peaceably, the last vestiges of authority were removed by agreement in 1933. Puerto Rico decided to remain with the United States practically on that island's own terms and today seems very happy with the choice. Also in 1898-99, the Samoa Islands were divided between the United States and Germany, and Hawaii decided to join the United States by annexation.

In 1901 occurred the Boxer Rebellion in China. For the relief of the besieged nationals of foreign powers within the walls of the British

---

[3]In the summer of 1961, General Aguinaldo, at the age of 92, was invited to attend the 15th anniversary celebration of the independence of the Philippine Republic. His health, however, did not permit his acceptance.

Legation in Peking (Peiping), a relief army, composed of American, British, French, German, Russian, and Japanese troops, fought its way through Tien-Tsin to the besieged people in Peking. Of the total indemnity paid by China, the less than 10% portion of it paid to the United States, 24 million dollars, was later remitted to China by Acts of Congress, and the money was used by China largely for educational purposes.[4]

While firearms in the hands of evil men are evil things, in the hands of people dedicated to independence and freedom, buoyed by the faith and hope of the world, these same weapons measure the difference between salvation and slavery. From the international record, it is evident that the United States has acted honorably. Not only that but with our weapons we have helped to encourage freedom for other peoples penned within their own frontiers by dictatorships; and we have supported peoples who found their frontiers crossed by those who would enslave them mentally, morally, or physically. But this aid had to be founded first on the will and determination of those same peoples to help themselves.

Unfortunately, mankind does not seem to be able to stand a long peace any more than it can stand long wars. The longest period of peace in the world's history appears to have been at the time of Christ — forty years during the reign of Augustus Caesar. Peace seems to breed laxity, luxury, personal rather than national security, venality, and trouble. Like ripe fruit, the next step is decay. We tend to worship the blush of maturity, the retention of status; while other people not so fortunate design to dispossess us. Yet if we consider this competition logically and historically, we must admit that it is good for us when we face it squarely. Thus we grow again.

"Eternal vigilance is the price of freedom." This means that we have to be vigilant in maintaining our moral and physical welfare as well as ready and willing to fight for freedom whether from threats outside our borders or decay from within.

[4]E. Benjamin Andrews, *History of the United States* (New York, 1914); David S. Muzzey, *The American People* (New York, 1932).

POSTLUDE

TRAILS HARMONIZE FOR PROGRESS
— THE HERITAGE

At this point we leave the trail in the development of firearms covering a long and troubled course from the primitive gunpowder of the 13th century to the refined smokeless powders ushering in the first World War of the 20th century. During those six hundred years wherein we have been following the course of fire, explosives, and mechanisms for their use, similar and parallel courses in other fields of human endeavor have been marching right along with us, exchanging ideas to mutual advantage, at the same time making independent discoveries of incalculable value to humanity. For more than three hundred and fifty years in America, inventions, new technical skills, and progress in the better use of natural resources have urged us forward. These are the trails that reveal man's strengths far more than his weaknesses.

But the resulting conquest and unification of a continent have required not only steel in firearms but also steel in men. From the Revolution through the Spanish-American War, Americans had to fight and work hard to maintain their own freedoms. They struggled with and took counsel with one another. Each had his own opinions, and with stern convictions of what was right and just he had the courage to fight and die for those convictions. Finally these Americans became real partners in government. Whatever security they had came only from opportunity, through their own efforts and their faith in God. They had no guarantees for success. That, they had to earn.

This vigorous, risky initiative, this self-reliance, this courage, and this independence — backed by integrity, upright character, and regardless of obstacles, the will to win — forged the steel in the men and women of America which can be eroded only by neglecting these basic parts of our heritage.

* * * *

"If a nation values anything more than freedom, it will lose its freedom; and the irony of it is, that if it is comfort or money that it values more, it will lose that too." — Somerset Maugham.

SELECTED GUN BOOK BIBLIOGRAPHY

BOOKS

Blackmore, Howard L. BRITISH MILITARY FIREARMS, 1650-1850. London: Herbert Jenkins, 1961.

Chapel, Charles Edward, GUN COLLECTING. New York: Coward-McCann, Inc., 1960.

Colts' Patent Fire Arms Manufacturing Company, 100th ANNIVERSARY FIRE ARMS MANUAL. Hartford, Conn.: Colts' Patent Fire Arms Manufacturing Company, 1936.

Dillin, John G. W., THE KENTUCKY RIFLE. Washington, D. C.: National Rifle Association of America, 1924.

Edwards, William B., THE STORY OF COLT'S REVOLVER. Harrisburg, Pa.: Stackpole, 1953.

Fuller, Claude E., SPRINGFIELD MUZZLE-LOADING SHOULDER ARMS. New York: Francis Bannerman Sons, 1930.

Gluckman, Arcadi, UNITED STATES MARTIAL PISTOLS AND REVOLV-ERS. Buffalo, N. Y.: Otto Ulbrich Company, 1939.

———, UNITED STATES MUSKETS, RIFLES, AND CARBINES. Buffalo, N. Y.: Otto Ulbrich Company, 1948.

Gluckman, Arcadi and L. D. Satterlee, AMERICAN GUN MAKERS. Harrisburg, Pa.: Stackpole, 1953.

Hanson, Charles E., Jr., THE NORTHWEST GUN. Lincoln: Nebraska State Historical Society, 1955, c1956, (Nebraska State Historical Society. Publications in Anthropology, no. 2)

———, THE PLAINS RIFLE. Harrisburg, Pa.: Stackpole, 1960.

Haven, Charles T. and Frank A. Belden, A HISTORY OF THE COLT REVOLVER AND THE OTHER ARMS MADE BY COLT'S PATENT FIREARMS MANUFACTURING COMPANY FROM 1836 TO 1940. New York: William Morrow and Company, 1940.

Held, Robert, THE AGE OF FIREARMS. New York: Harper, 1957.

Hicks, James E., NOTES ON UNITED STATES ORDNANCE. Mount Vernon, N. Y.: The Author, c1940. 2 vols.

Lewis, Berkeley R., SMALL ARMS AND AMMUNITION IN U. S. SERVICE. Washington, D. C.: Smithsonian Institution, 1956.

Parsons, John E., SMITH & WESSON REVOLVERS. New York: William Morrow & Company, 1957.

Russell, Carl P., GUNS ON THE EARLY FRONTIERS; A HISTORY OF FIREARMS FROM COLONIAL TIMES THROUGH THE YEARS OF THE WESTERN FUR TRADE. Berkeley: University of California Press, 1957.

Satterlee, L. D., A CATALOG OF FIREARMS FOR THE COLLECTOR. Detroit: Privately Printed, 1939.

Sawyer, Charles W., FIREARMS IN AMERICAN HISTORY, 1600-1800. Boston: The Author, c1910.

————, FIREARMS IN AMERICAN HISTORY: THE REVOLVER, 1800-1911. Boston: The Arms Company, c1911.

————, OUR RIFLES. Boston: The Cornhill Company, c1920.

Serven, James E., COLT FIREARMS, 1836-1954. Santa Ana, Calif.: Serven Gun Room, 1954.

Sharpe, Philip B., THE RIFLE IN AMERICA. New York: William Morrow & Company, 1938.

Williamson, Harold F., WINCHESTER, THE GUN THAT WON THE WEST. Washington, D. C.: Combat Forces Press, 1952.

CATALOGS

Robert Abels, Inc., 860 Lexington Avenue, New York 21, New York. $1.00

Norm Flayderman, 44 West Putnam Avenue, Greenwich, Connecticut. $1.00

Jackson Arms, 6209-G Hillcrest Street, Dallas, Texas. $1.00

INDEX

using percussion lock, e.g. Hawken rifle
Perkin, Joseph 29
Petersburg, Va. 60
Pettengill revolver 75
Philadelphia 42
Philippine Insurrection 78-81
Philippine Islands 78, 80, 84
Pickett, George E. 61
Pin-fire cartridge 47, 50, 76
Pirates and piracy 25, 31
Pistol 24, 29n3, 50-51, 54, 59, 75, 77
  Automatic 77
  Duelling 26, 28
  Flintlock 24, 30, 34, 38
  "Horse" 24, 38
  Metallic cartridge 49n2, 50, 67-69, 75-76
  Multi-shot 37, 40, 54
  Pepperbox 40, 42, 75
  Percussion 30, 37, 40, 54
  Single-shot 49n2, 59
  see also Revolver; and names of specific pistols, e.g. Volcanic magazine pistol
Plains rifle 36
Plainsman 36
Ploughboy (horse) 27
"Poison Bullet" 80
Portland, Me. 31
Powder, see Gunpowder
Powder horn 9, 18, 22
Powell, James 64
Prescott, William 18
Prescott percussion revolver 54
Primer 46, 50
  Center-fire 49n2
  Disc 48
  Maynard tape primer 43n12, 52-53
  Percussion 50, 52
  Tape 43n12, 52-53
Priming powder 3n2, 5-7
  see also Gunpowder
Puerto Rico 78, 84
Pyrites 1, 5-6

Quebec 12, 14, 21
Queen Anne's War 9

Rall, Johann Gottlieb 21
Range 62
  of musket 8
  of revolver 72, 75
  of rifle 8, 23, 44, 60, 63-65, 72
Rappahannock Forge 24

Reformado 80
Regiment of Mississippians, see Mississippi Regiment
Regiment of Mounted Rifles, see Mounted Rifles, Regiment of
Remington, E. 42, 43n12
Remington Arms Co., Inc. 54, 58, 75
Remington carbine 56n5, 79
Remington revolver 54, 68, 75-76
Remington rifle 75, 79-80
Reno, Marcus A. 70-71
Repeater 52, 65-67, 71, 75
Republican River, Arikaree Fork 65-67
Revolution, American, see American Revolution
Revolver 37, 39-44, 47-48, 50, 54, 59, 65-69, 71-72, 75-76, 79, 81
  Flintlock 37
  Metallic cartridge 50, 54, 67-69, 76
  Multi-shot 40, 54, 79
  Pepperbox 40, 42, 75
  Percussion 37, 40, 42, 48, 54-55, 65-66
  see also names of specific revolvers, e.g. Colt revolver
Revolving rifle 39-41, 55
Richmond Armory 58
Rifle 8, 10, 12-15, 17, 19-26, 29-32, 34-44, 46, 48, 51, 53, 55-67, 71, 75-76, 78-82
  Effectiveness 23-24, 60-61
  Flintlock 14n4, 21-22, 30-32, 34-35
  Magazine 76, 79, 81
  Metallic cartridge 49n2, 56-57, 62, 64
  Model 1803 29-32, 42
  Model 1814 42
  Model 1841 42-43, 46
  Model 1855 43n12, 53
  Model 1866 62-64
  Model 1903 81-82
  Percussion 26, 34-36, 40, 42, 46, 48-49
  Repeating 52, 65-67, 71, 75
  Revolving 39-41, 55
  see also names of specific rifles, e.g. Pennsylvania rifle
Rifled musket 43n12, 53
Rifling 8, 23, 52, 62, 82
Rim-fire cartridge 47-48, 49n2, 50-51, 53, 57, 62, 68, 77
Rio Grande 43
Robbins & Lawrence 42
Rochester, N. Y. 39